Managing
Public Debt

Managing Public Debt

From Diagnostics to Reform Implementation

THE WORLD BANK
Washington, D.C.

ISBN-10: 0-8213-6872-9
ISBN-13: 978-0-8213-6872-5
eISBN-10: 0-8213-6873-7
eISBN-13: 978-0-8213-6873-2
DOI: 10.1596/978-0-8213-6872-5

Library of Congress Cataloging-in-Publication Data
Managing public debt : from diagnostics to reform implementation.
    p. cm.
  ISBN-13: 978-0-8213-6872-5
  ISBN-10: 0-8213-6872-9
  ISBN-10: 0-8213-6873-7 (electronic)
  1. Debts, Public—Management.   2. Debts, Public—Developing countries.
I. World Bank.
  HJ8015.M26 2007
  352.4'5091724--dc22

2006036974

CONTENTS

TABLES

PREFACE

This is the first volume of a study on the insights from a 12-country pilot program on public debt management and domestic government debt market development. The pilot program was undertaken by a joint team from the World Bank's Banking and Debt Management Group of the Treasury and Corporate Governance and Capital Markets Department. The second volume covers insights on domestic government debt market development.

Managing Public Debt was prepared by Phillip Anderson and Eriko Togo of the Treasury at the World Bank. It summarizes the analysis and findings of a series of country assessment reports and reform plans covering the 12 countries that participated in the pilot program. The book draws heavily on the contributions of World Bank Treasury staff who took part in the preparation of the country reports. These include Phillip Anderson, Elizabeth Currie, Fred Jensen, Lars Jessen, Tomas Magnusson, and Antonio Velandia-Rubiano. Extensive comments were provided by Anderson Caputo Silva and Dimitri Vittas. Background research was prepared by Weenarin Lulitanonda. George Iden, Rodolfo Maino, and Brian Olden of the International Monetary Fund contributed to three country reports. External consultants include Fred Ruhakana of Macroeconomic and Financial Management Institute of Eastern and Southern Africa, and Mike Williams. Extensive support was provided by the country directors and staff from the regional vice presidencies of the World Bank. Peer review on earlier drafts was provided by Homi Kharas, Sudarashan Gooptu, Vikram Nehru, and Stijn Claessens (World Bank); Otavio Ladeira and Rodrigo Siveira of the Brazilian Treasury; and Guillermo Garrido of the Peruvian Ministry of Finance and Economy. Editorial service was provided by David Cheney. The authors would also like to thank the authorities in the 12 pilot countries for participating in the pilot program and providing invaluable inputs to the process.

EXECUTIVE SUMMARY

High-quality public debt management plays a critical role in reducing developing countries' vulnerability to financial crises. Good debt management encompasses sound risk and cash management, effective coordination with fiscal and monetary policy, good governance, and adequate institutional and staff capacity. With these in place, governments can develop and implement effective medium-term debt management strategies. Effective implementation of debt management strategies also requires a developed domestic government debt market, which is discussed in *Developing the Domestic Government Debt Market*.

The World Bank and the International Monetary Fund (IMF) have taken steps to help countries improve their public debt management and domestic debt market development by disseminating sound practices in these areas—notably by publishing "Guidelines for Public Debt Management" (World Bank and IMF 2001b) and *Developing Government Bond Markets: A Handbook* (World Bank and IMF 2001a). However, moving from a set of general principles to a program of concrete reform is not easy. The World Bank and the IMF thus sought to extend their assistance by setting up, in 2002, a joint pilot program to help countries design the relevant reform and capacity-building programs.

The 12 countries participating in the program—Bulgaria, Colombia, Costa Rica, Croatia, Indonesia, Kenya, Lebanon, Nicaragua, Pakistan, Sri Lanka, Tunisia, and Zambia—are geographically and economically diverse. Their experiences illustrate the challenges and elements necessary to make progress in public debt management and domestic government debt market development.

To assess the experience of the pilot countries with public debt management, the pilot program's findings are grouped into five categories.

DEBT MANAGEMENT STRATEGIES

An explicit public debt management strategy puts into operation the overall objectives for debt management and sets out a medium-term framework for how the government will manage the composition of debt. A framework should be developed to enable debt managers to identify and manage the trade-offs between expected cost and risk in the government debt portfolio. This is supported by a quantification of risk, including stress tests of the debt portfolio based on the economic and financial shocks to which the country is potentially exposed. A good debt management strategy must spell out the nature of the constraints and provide a rationale for the chosen approach.

The debt managers in most pilot countries had a good understanding of the key risks of their debt portfolios, and government borrowing was shaped by implicit strategies that were based on a general understanding of the cost-risk trade-offs. Although such approaches have largely been reasonable, the lack of an overall explicit strategy based on thorough analysis has been limiting in a number of respects. First, it has meant that there was only a partial understanding of the trade-offs being made for possible cost outcomes. Second, it has allowed for inconsistencies in the management of different parts of the debt portfolio, resulting in actions to reduce risks or costs for one subportfolio conflicting with those of another. Third, it has allowed choices about borrowing to be inconsistent through time, because it has allowed short-term expediency to dominate (to reduce budgetary costs) the medium-term goal of prudent risk management, or the priorities of monetary policy implementation to be too readily accepted.

A strategy can be developed gradually, with quality improvements over time as capacity is strengthened and more analysis is undertaken. A useful first step is to codify and document the rationale and existing processes that define the composition of the debt. The strategy can range from simply having an intended direction for the debt portfolio to specific targets or a borrowing program, usually expressed with ranges. For the pilot countries with severely constrained funding choices—especially those limited to highly concessional borrowing (where terms are dictated by the creditor and where domestic debt markets are limited)—a more general strategy is usually better. But for some risks, harder targets may be preferable.

COORDINATION OF DEBT STRATEGY WITH OTHER POLICIES

Improving the quality of public debt management can achieve only so much; ultimately, fiscal policy determines the borrowing requirement and is the main influence on the stock of debt over time. To best support measures for improving public debt management, governments should thus have in place similarly sound frameworks for fiscal policy.

Coordination between debt management and monetary policy is also important, especially in countries with less developed domestic government debt markets. Conflict between debt management and monetary policy, or the potential for such conflict, was seen as likely to occur in the pilot countries where the central bank takes a leading role in managing domestic debt. The central bank may encounter pressure to reduce government debt servicing costs by providing direct financing, or to maintain interest rates at lower levels than desirable for price stability. The central bank's leading role in debt management is often the result of limited capacity in finance ministries, and efforts to change this can only occur slowly. Shorter-term measures include agreements between central banks and ministries of finance that clarify decision-making rules with respect to domestic debt management as well as greater transparency in implementing monetary policy.

Poor coordination with cash management also hinders effective debt management. In a number of pilot-program countries, the timing of domestic borrowing was determined by the government's cash flow needs, because there was no active cash management or instruments to smooth the short-run peaks and troughs in the government's cash flow. Thus, the size and composition of government bond auctions varied greatly from month to month. This unpredictability, in turn, undermined efforts to develop the domestic government debt market. To improve management of domestic borrowing, reform efforts may need to extend into the areas of budget execution and cash management.

Lack of progress in coordinating debt management with fiscal and monetary management, as well as with cash management in several pilot countries, has highlighted that reforming debt management in isolation can achieve limited success and that more comprehensive reforms can be mutually reinforcing.

GOOD GOVERNANCE

The governance structure supporting public debt management should delineate clear roles and responsibilities for the institutions involved, be guided by checks and balances, and include clear reporting lines.

Most pilot-program countries met the minimum requirement of having legislation that clarified the authority to borrow in the name of the government. This authority, however, typically resided in a number of separate laws, mandated responsibilities for debt management to a number of different entities, and specified different processes and levels of authority for borrowing. Although most countries get by, these arrangements are frequently inefficient and sometimes require inventive maneuvering for the system to function. The institutional and political difficulties associated with legislative change often hampered the formulation of new laws and amendments, but some pilot countries used secondary regulations to implement more urgent initiatives.

Management of public debt in the pilot countries was split across a number of different departments, typically including ministries of finance, central banks, and economics and planning ministries. The dispersion of responsibility tended to reflect the source of the borrowing. Changes in institutional responsibilities were frequently recommended to move debt management closer to sound practices, but these changes have proven difficult to implement.

A major challenge for achieving accountability has been to obtain adequate independent assurance about reporting and about the processes used by public debt managers. In some countries, external auditors have publicly called for improvements to the management of public debt, including institutional arrangements, the need for a strategy, and better accounting. In others, external audits were confined to financial statements, which lack information on the stock of debt. In all countries, the specialized nature of transactions in financial markets called for an external auditor competent in treasury accounting and able to provide assurances about the risk and control environment in the debt management unit.

CAPACITY: STAFF AND DEBT MANAGEMENT SYSTEMS

Public debt management requires staff with a combination of financial market, economics, and public policy skills. The recruitment and retention of skilled and experienced staff is one of the greatest challenges for improving the quality of public debt management in most pilot-program countries. Unless this is addressed, significant efforts by governments and donors will have, at best, only a transitory impact.

Building staff capacity is a challenge in many public sector reform programs, however. Two common problems were evident in the pilot countries:

- Public sector laws, rules, and practices in several countries (especially low salaries) impeded the recruitment and retention of sufficient staff, or those with the appropriate mix of skills.

▓ Staff turnover was high, due partly to the fact that as civil service staff gained skills and experience in public debt management, they left for better-paying positions in the private sector.

Nevertheless, the pilot countries have implemented a variety of measures to build staff capacity, including creating opportunities for short-term external assignments, improving incentives for career progression, and making use of existing public sector capacity-building programs and international support networks. These have been supplemented with the use of resident advisors, external consultants, and secondments from the central bank, as well as relaxing human resources management restrictions and establishing islands of excellence.

Also important for good debt management are sound debt recording systems; many donors have focused their considerable development assistance in this area. Still, a few pilot countries continue to struggle with basic debt recording and reporting. This may be due to a focus on system installation, while less attention is paid to user needs and capacity building for data input and maintaining and using the system. A more common challenge is the integration of (domestic and external) debt data from separate systems reflecting separate institutional arrangements. Although not insurmountable, the required workarounds can be slow and entail double entry of data, which increases operational risk. As a result, a complete picture of a country's debt may be difficult to obtain and the ability to extract data for analysis may be impeded. Also, as countries gain market access and use a broader array of instruments, their needs frequently exceed their systems' capabilities.

Rather than embark on major systems projects, a number of countries in the pilot program opted to improve information technology systems by taking smaller steps, including making better use of existing systems and developing better interfaces to produce more easily consolidated debt reporting outputs.

DESIGNING AND IMPLEMENTING REFORMS

The outcome of the diagnostic reports in the 12 countries supported the premise that a comprehensive diagnostic was necessary. The diagnostic not only captures the main building blocks of debt management, but it also identifies the interrelationships with macroeconomic policies, the overall governance environment, and the level of development of the domestic government debt market. An analysis of these interactions helps identify the nature of trade-offs across different policies, priorities for reform, and the possible consequences of reform in some areas.

In general, reform programs that reflected country-specific priorities, the prevailing political climate, technical difficulty, and capacity constraints have seen greater incremental progress toward implementation than those that laid out the first-best solutions that were impractical to implement. In addition, reform plans that incorporate medium-term institutional development and capacity building while taking into account immediate constraints, have helped keep the bigger picture in sight.

As is the case for reforms in many areas, the most important factor in sustaining the reform has been "ownership" by the government. A second factor that has proved important in sustaining reforms is the establishment of an institutional environment that can facilitate change. This includes the existence of an effective leader or "champion" of change and mechanisms to bridge across organizations. Most pilot countries that made progress had an identifiable leader, but a common problem was key person risk. Finally, it was noted that the debt management reform process may be more effectively sustained by integrating it into broader programs, such as public financial management reforms.

The pilot program also had implications for providers of assistance. For example, public debt management does not fit neatly into traditional sectoral categories. Thus, diagnostics that have a principal focus on the financial sector, for example, might examine debt management from the perspective of its relation to financial sector vulnerability rather than examining the issues that a comprehensive diagnostic would cover. In addition, diagnostics should be routinely followed up by helping countries initiate the reforms. Also, because of the long-term nature of reforms of this type, donors will be most effective if they are able to stay involved in the process on a continuous basis, rather than through one-off engagements. As with any project or program, donor coordination is important to ensure that all components are covered, but not duplicated.

Introduction

The financial crises in East Asia, the Russian Federation, and Latin America in the 1990s and the early 2000s drew attention to the quality of public debt management in developing countries, and to the role that deeper and more efficient domestic government debt markets can play in reducing financial vulnerability. As a result, officials, academics, financial institutions, and multilateral agencies have stepped up their efforts to promote reform and build capacity in these areas.

The World Bank and the International Monetary Fund (IMF) have contributed to the effort by developing and disseminating sound practices in the areas of public debt management and domestic government debt market development, particularly through the *Guidelines for Public Debt Management* (the Guidelines) and *Developing Government Bond Markets: A Handbook* (the Handbook). While these offer general guidance and are necessarily idealized, they present a set of principles on which there is broad international agreement. For example, government debt managers from some 30 countries commented on the initial draft of the Guidelines, and more than 300 representatives from 122 countries attended five conferences and provided feedback before the Guidelines were finalized. Thus, they provide a sound basis for the development of reforms in countries at different levels of development.

Still, the process of moving from a set of general principles to a program of concrete reforms and capacity building in a particular country is anything but straightforward. For example, many Financial Sector Assessment Program reports underscore the need for improvements in debt management and domestic government debt market development. In general, however, the World Bank and the IMF have not actively extended their assistance to follow up on these recommendations.[1] Recognizing this, a joint World Bank–IMF pilot program including 12 countries was initiated in 2002.[2]

The 12 countries in the pilot program—Bulgaria, Colombia, Costa Rica, Croatia, Indonesia, Kenya, Lebanon, Nicaragua, Pakistan, Sri Lanka, Tunisia, and Zambia—are geographically diverse and represent countries at different stages of economic and financial development.[3] This allows for the exploration of commonalities and differences in applying principles for sound debt management and market development across a spectrum of countries.

The diversity of the pilot countries is illustrated in table 1.1 below.

The purpose of the pilot program is to assist countries in designing a reform and capacity-building program in public debt management and domestic government debt market development. For public debt management, the ultimate objective is to help countries so that the governance

TABLE 1.1   Key Indicators for 12 Pilot-Program Countries, year end 2005

Country	Population (millions)	GDP per capita (US$)	Public debt to GDP ratio (percent)	Real GDP growth (annual percent)
Bulgaria	7.7	3,442	31.9	5.5
Colombia	45.6	2,682	47.4	5.1
Costa Rica	4.3	4,491	56.1	5.9
Croatia	4.4	8,418	45.5	4.1
Indonesia	220.6	1,302	46.5	5.6
Kenya	33.4	464	50.1	4.7
Lebanon	3.6	6,210	175.0	1.0
Nicaragua	5.5	895	136.0	4.0
Pakistan	155.8	711	69.0	7.0
Sri Lanka	19.6	1,199	93.9	5.9
Tunisia	10.0	2,862	58.4	4.2
Zambia	11.7	622	68.5	5.1

Sources: Data on population and GDP per capita are based on World Bank (2006); public debt to GDP ratio is based on selected IMF Article IV consultations (IMF 2003, 2004c, 2004d, 2005b) and government Web sites; and real GDP growth is based on IMF (2006b).

arrangements, internal processes, resources, and staff capacity are in place to enable them to

■ develop a medium-term debt management strategy with yearly updates, based on a sound analysis of cost and risk, taking account of macroeconomic and market constraints; and
■ implement the strategy efficiently, while managing operational risk in a prudent manner.

To facilitate the implementation of a debt management strategy, another explicit goal has been to promote the development of the domestic government debt market by creating the conditions for developing money markets, primary markets, the investor base, secondary markets, custody and settlement systems, and debt market regulation.

To help countries move from a set of principles to a program of concrete reforms and capacity building, the pilot program built on an initial comprehensive diagnostic of country needs. The diagnostic focused on both public debt management and domestic government debt market development and covered all areas that had potentially important policy implications. In addition to the initial diagnostic, the pilot program envisioned two additional stages: formulating a reform plan and implementing the proposed reforms.

Three basic considerations motivated this approach:

1. Because of the high degree of complementarity and interaction between public debt management and domestic government debt market development, it was felt that simultaneous examination of the challenges facing each of these areas would result in better-informed diagnostic reports and more effective reform plans.
2. Within each of these two major areas, it was necessary to examine the full range of relevant issues. For example, to develop a medium-term debt management strategy, addressing the enabling environment was important. This included the governance and legal framework, coordination with other macroeconomic policies, and the quality of internal operations—including risk management, staff capacity, and information systems. Shortcomings and constraints in any of these areas could hinder the development of more efficient strategies. Similarly, a comprehensive diagnostic approach was needed to identify obstacles to the development of important components of efficient domestic government debt markets, such as money markets, primary

and secondary debt markets, the investor base, settlement and custody systems, and debt market regulation.

3. While the above considerations justified a comprehensive approach in the assessment stage, the design of reform plans and implementation programs had to take full account of the stage of development of both institutions and markets, including the institutional capacity of central banks and other state entities. The complexity of debt policies and markets implied that reform plans would take a long time to implement and needed to reflect initial conditions in each country, as well as the existing capacity to adopt basic policy measures.

The pilot program was resourced with World Bank staff from the Treasury Vice Presidency and the Finance and Private Sector Development Vice Presidency, with support from IMF staff or consultants participating on four assessment missions. World Bank regional staff as well as external consultants contributed in specific areas or countries. The staff involved in the program had expertise and practical experience in most aspects of public debt management and domestic government debt market development, and in providing assistance to a wide range of World Bank clients.

Participation in the program was open to governments fully committed to building capacity and to adopting reforms in the areas of public debt management and domestic government debt market development. In some countries, reform was already under way, but the authorities were attracted by the broad scope of the pilot program and wished to take stock and receive advice on the next steps. This publication documents the insights from the 12 pilot countries. It is based on input from the individual country diagnostics, reform plans, and ongoing work to support the implementation of the reform process.

The implementation of reforms is at an early stage in the 12 pilot-program countries. Given the comprehensive nature of the programs and, particularly, the need in some cases for institutional change, it will be years before outcomes can be fully evaluated. Although work is still in progress and an evaluation of the final outcomes of the pilot program would be premature, considerable experience has been gained from the work to date, which will be useful both to countries considering reforms in these areas and to organizations and people providing technical assistance. The experience to date has yielded a deeper understanding of common challenges, of how countries have gone about moving toward sound practices, and of the measures that have been easy to implement and those that have not.

The pilot program does not address the important issue of public debt sustainability, on the assumption that this is addressed separately in each country, mainly through a framework for sound fiscal policy. Nevertheless, interactions are addressed because more efficient debt management and a more efficient domestic government debt market should lower financial risks and over time lower borrowing costs—thus facilitating the attainment of more sustainable levels of public debt. Also not addressed explicitly are positive externalities for overall welfare arising from an efficient domestic government debt market. For example, the provision of a benchmark yield curve facilitates the issuance of corporate and mortgage bonds as well as the promotion of asset securitization. Liquid benchmark issues may also constitute efficient risk-hedging instruments.

Because the focus of the pilot program is to draw on the experiences of the pilot countries to illustrate how governments are transitioning from the diagnostic stage to designing reform plans and implementing them, readers are directed to other sources for more extensive descriptions of sound practices on individual topics or themes.

This study follows a thematic approach to the analysis rather than a country-by-country approach.[4] Each chapter consists of three subsections, beginning with a brief statement of sound practices, thematic diagnostics of the country situations, followed by a description of the reform experiences and examples of the actions taken by the governments to implement reform.[5] *Developing the Domestic Government Debt Market* discusses domestic government debt market development topics. It covers money markets, primary markets, the investor base, secondary markets, custody and settlement, and debt market regulation.

Following this introductory chapter, chapter 2 begins by describing and drawing insights from the experiences to date of the countries moving from diagnostics to reform implementation, with a focus on the processes and factors that have helped countries move toward addressing weaknesses in public debt management.

Chapter 3 addresses debt management strategy and risk management. It looks at the risks and the constraints faced by the 12 pilot countries. Few of the countries had formal, documented debt management strategies, which reduced the probability of consistent, long-run management of the public debt.

Chapter 4 discusses the coordination between debt management, fiscal policy, monetary policy, and cash management. A number of pilot countries have high debt levels and sustainability concerns, and domestic government debt markets in most are not well developed. This complicates the achievement of a degree of separation between public debt management and macroeconomic policies.

Chapter 5 considers the critical importance of good governance in developing and implementing a prudent debt management strategy. It notes that the dispersed organizational arrangements and supporting legal framework pose difficult challenges in many pilot-program countries. Strong accountability and transparency are important, given the size of the debt portfolios in these countries and their potential to affect macroeconomic outcomes, financial stability, and corruption.

Well-qualified and experienced staff are vital for the sound management of public debt. Chapter 6 finds that inadequate capacity and poor management of internal operations is a key problem in many pilot-program countries. These countries need information technology systems that securely and accurately record their debt and provide required reporting and analysis. They also need controls similar to those in financial institutions.

Designing and Implementing Reforms: An Overview

A key objective of the pilot program was to develop a better under-standing of the process of reform, specifically, how to move from a set of principles to the implementation of an explicit program of reforms and capacity building in public debt management. We approached this in three phases by

- conducting a comprehensive diagnostic,
- designing the reform program, and
- initiating specific actions.

Although implementation is still in various stages in the 12 pilot coun-tries, and an assessment of the effectiveness of particular reform pro-grams would be premature, this chapter describes and draws insights from the experiences to date of the countries at each stage. Thus, the focus is on the processes and factors that have helped countries move toward addressing weaknesses in public debt management. The chapter also pro-vides views on the role of external providers of assistance.

THE DIAGNOSTIC STAGE

The outcome of the diagnostic reports in the 12 countries supported the premise that a comprehensive diagnostic was necessary. Not only does the diagnostic capture the main building blocks of debt management, it also identifies the interrelationships with macroeconomic policies, the overall governance environment, and the level of development of the domestic government debt market. An analysis of these interactions helps identify the trade-offs across different policies, priorities for reform, and the possible consequences of reform in some areas.

A thorough understanding of the macroeconomic situation and the relationship with debt management is crucial because debt management reforms tend to be more effective where a credible macroeconomic framework is in place and where stability has been achieved or is progressing. An analysis focused narrowly on debt management, which does not take into account or is inconsistent with the overall macroeconomic framework, might lead to unrealistic recommendations. In addition, presentation to the authorities of the broader policy context provides for a realistic assessment of what can be achieved by public debt management reform.

In pilot countries with high debt levels and negative debt dynamics, fiscal consolidation was a priority (Croatia and Sri Lanka). In more extreme cases, where debt levels had become unsustainable, more drastic action was necessary, including debt forgiveness (Nicaragua and Zambia), debt renegotiation with creditors (Nicaragua), or voluntary action by the international community to reduce the debt burden (Lebanon). High public debt levels and the associated interest costs sharpen the trade-off between reducing costs in the short run and managing the financial risks in the medium term. Therefore, poor fiscal management can result in riskier debt portfolios and can increase vulnerability to shocks (for example, Costa Rica 1999–2001, Sri Lanka 2000–01).[1]

High and volatile inflation must be reduced before significant progress can be made in lowering risks in the domestic debt portfolio. All pilot countries achieved reasonable inflation outcomes before the pilot program and were seeking to establish policy credibility over the medium term. Pilot countries were aware that separating debt management from monetary policy implementation enhances central bank credibility. However, in a number of these countries, doing so has proven to be a challenge, particularly where the central bank also issues significant debt in its own name (Costa Rica and Nicaragua) and where capacity in the finance ministry is weak (Kenya, Zambia, and Sri Lanka). In the former case, recapitalization of the central bank or transferring liabilities to the government were necessary before the central bank could stop issuing significant debt.[2] Given the impact on the governments' finances, recapitalization or liability transfer are likely to occur slowly and the development of reform options had to take this into account.

The nature of the overall governance environment should be considered when assessing the state of public debt management. If the corruption level is high, the chances of reforming public debt management are slim. For example, in Kenya, ministerial approval of illegal transactions, combined with the lack of enforcement of independent auditing and accountability arrangements, demonstrated the need for broader action. Reforms of public debt management are now under way, following the revelation of the governance scandal and the arrest and replacement of senior-level staff.[3]

The level of development of the domestic debt market also has a crucial impact on debt management. In the pilot countries, issues such as the lack of a predictable and transparent primary market (Costa Rica, Pakistan, Sri Lanka, and Tunisia), dominance of commercial banks in government securities (Bulgaria, Croatia, Indonesia, Lebanon, Pakistan, Tunisia, and Zambia), poor risk management by commercial banks (Colombia and Tunisia), lack of development of contractual savings (most of the 12 countries), and lack of large and liquid benchmark issues and active trading in the secondary market (most of the 12 countries) all had implications for the management of domestic debt.[4] A comprehensive diagnostic that examines these interrelationships helps identify a realistic medium-term debt management strategy. Furthermore, the development of a related set of reforms may lessen the impact of these constraints and allow governments to reduce costs and better manage risks in the public debt portfolio.

A comprehensive diagnostic also helps reveal weaknesses caused by institutional arrangements for debt management. For example, in Costa Rica, Indonesia, Kenya, Lebanon, Nicaragua, Pakistan, Sri Lanka, and Zambia, where debt management responsibilities are scattered across institutions, analysis of the process in its entirety highlighted inconsistencies in strategies and inefficiencies arising from the duplication of functions. In some countries, the division of responsibilities was mandated by laws, or even in the constitution. Therefore, the practicality and time frame of amending the legal framework had to be considered if consolidation of debt management functions was to be recommended. A narrower approach, perhaps focused on improving the management of one type of debt (domestic borrowing, for example), may worsen organizational fragmentation.[5]

Thanks to greater international focus on sound debt management principles—such as the wide dissemination of the *Guidelines for Public Debt Management*—the authorities in many pilot countries understood the main challenges identified in the diagnostic report. Nevertheless, the comprehensive approach was valued because it was the first time the full set of issues related to the management of all public debt had been analyzed.

DESIGNING REFORMS

The dissemination of the diagnostic report in each country set the scene for the design of a reform program and prioritization of reforms. Dissemination of the report brought together players from different parts of government to discuss priorities, assess feasibility and technical difficulty, and establish a clear division of labor. In some pilot countries (Costa Rica, Indonesia, Kenya, Lebanon, Sri Lanka, and Zambia), it provided a forum to address interinstitutional differences, build a consensus for reform, and set up coordination mechanisms.

Most of the pilot countries have formulated reform plans of some type, although content and detail vary. The plans range from those consisting of a list of activities with broad timelines (Indonesia); to those in which the authorities identified priority actions in the context of a broader set of reforms being undertaken at the finance ministry (Lebanon); to those drafted by an appointed project team that embarked on a detailed planning process, identifying critical paths and accountabilities for the various components (Sri Lanka), or tasks for the coordination committee to design a debt management strategy (Costa Rica).[6]

In reviewing progress to date in the pilot countries, the comprehensiveness of any reform plan has not been a good predictor of successful outcomes because, to some extent, reform is a process and plans are revised, often as a result of political changes. For example, in Indonesia the timeline for institutional change was accelerated within one year after a change in minister. In Sri Lanka, despite detailed and careful planning, the authorities decided not to proceed, following a change in government. In Costa Rica, little action has been taken because of a delay in securing follow-up financing.[7] Tunisia did not draft a reform plan beyond what was prepared for a grant application before the pilot project, but it took actions based on the recommendations in the diagnostic report.

Nevertheless, certain elements in designing reforms seem to correlate with success in moving from the diagnostic stage to implementation. In particular, reform programs that reflected country-specific priorities, the prevailing political climate, technical difficulty, and capacity constraints resulted in greater incremental progress than those that laid out the first-best solutions that were impractical to implement. These reform experiences are best characterized as "good fit" rather than "best practice." In addition, reform plans that incorporate medium-term institutional development and capacity building while taking into account immediate constraints have helped keep the bigger picture in sight, thus helping governments identify opportunities to implement more-ambitious reforms.

Thus, few generalizations can be made about the sequencing of public debt management reforms. The basic building blocks that must come first are building capacity in the back office and establishing reliable debt recording systems so that debt can be serviced in a timely manner without reliance on lenders' notifications, and so that accurate and frequent reporting can be produced. While most countries already had these elements in place, Kenya and Zambia did not.

Beyond these steps, sequencing varied. For example, in Indonesia, Lebanon, and Tunisia, reforming the legal framework was judged to be difficult at an early stage; however, in Bulgaria, Croatia, and Nicaragua, legal reform was implemented first. Similarly, while Indonesia and Zambia initially decided to delay organizational reform, Colombia, Costa Rica, Croatia, and Kenya saw it as a necessary and feasible first step.[8]

Comprehensive institutional and legal reforms have not been a prerequisite for developing an overall debt management strategy across institutional boundaries—several pilot countries have demonstrated that significant progress can be made without such reform. Indeed, much can be achieved through the formation of a working group or coordination committee (Costa Rica and Indonesia) or by establishing islands of excellence with special budget and technical support to conduct analysis (Indonesia and Lebanon).

Experience also suggests, however, that such partial solutions, usually not first best, have risks and that the longer-term consequences should be carefully considered. For example, between 1996 and 1998, Colombia had a coordination committee to develop a debt management strategy, but the committee stopped meeting as key members resigned from the ministry of finance or the central bank; this ended further reviews of the strategy. In Kenya, capacity built in the 1990s was lost as trained staff left the ministry of finance; there was no institutional framework to maintain capacity. Similarly, where legal reforms were difficult, use of secondary legislation proved useful for avoiding delays in implementing reforms, but temporarily added to the already complicated and fragmented legal frameworks (Colombia and Indonesia). In Pakistan, the establishment of a new debt management coordination unit added to the already scattered organizational arrangements. (Other examples and details of how the countries have approached sequencing reform program components are covered in chapters 3–6.)

Finally, poorly designed reform programs can be costly. For example, Croatia implemented a public financial management system with a debt management module without prior study of the users' functional requirements. Neither the vendor, nor the government at the time, knew what a debt management system should look like and each had different expectations for the contributions of the other. Along with long delays and budgetary overruns, operational risk continued to increase from the aging of the old debt management system (which did not meet the evolving needs of the debt manager) and the lack of system support.

SUSTAINING THE REFORM PROCESS

Because reform in public debt management and domestic government debt market development are processes rather than one-off events, sustaining reform programs over time has been a key challenge. What were some of the critical factors that helped the 12 pilot countries sustain the reform process?

As with reform in many areas, the most important factor has been the government's commitment to the reform.[9] Indeed, a commitment to reform was a condition for participation in the pilot program and confirmation of commitment was sought at the outset. The stated motivations for reform varied: In Costa Rica and Sri Lanka, it was the central banks' desire to devolve debt management responsibilities to the ministry of finance, and in the meantime to develop greater coordination in the development of debt strategies. The Heavily Indebted Poor Countries (HIPC)[10] completion point and a new debt law in Nicaragua generated awareness of the need for more strategic improvements to public debt management. Bulgaria, Indonesia, and Tunisia wanted to build on previous achievements to improve public debt management and develop domestic government debt markets, as well as to improve macroeconomic management. In Croatia and Lebanon, deteriorating macroeconomic conditions were a motivating factor, while in Colombia, the trigger was a local crisis in the domestic government debt market.

When the government's commitment to the reform program diminished, its progress soon stopped. For example, in Sri Lanka, the key players had a change of heart about the direction of reform after encountering problems such as lack of capacity in the finance ministry and a change of government. In Nicaragua and Zambia, the diminished urgency of reform following the completion of the HIPC debt-forgiveness process lessened country ownership. In Lebanon, fractious politics and changes of government rendered impractical the more ambitious aspects of reform.

A second important factor in sustaining reform is the existence of a supportive institutional environment. The existence of an effective leader or "champion" of change as well as mechanisms to coordinate across organizations are particularly important. Most pilot countries making progress had an identifiable leader, but common problems were key-person risk or the key person being overloaded with competing reform priorities and day-to-day responsibilities. Perhaps the clearest example was in Nicaragua, where the departure of a senior manager who was able to push the reform agenda forward effectively stalled the reform process.

To help ensure that organizations cooperated in implementing reforms, senior officials in a number of countries mandated the formation of teams. In Indonesia, a ministerial decree was issued establishing a collective project team. In Kenya, the Permanent Secretary signed a memorandum of understanding committing the finance ministry to set up a project, comprising a project team and a high-level steering committee, with the mandate to design a detailed program of reforms and capacity building in public debt management and domestic debt market development. In Sri Lanka, a dedicated establishment team, headed by a director, was set up to prepare for a new public debt management office.

Finally, the debt management reform process can be more effectively sustained by integrating it into broader programs, such as public sector or public financial management reforms. Such integration helps ensure project sustainability and continuity through financing, support by experts, and project supervision. Another benefit derives if these broader programs address such fundamental problems as civil service or public financial management weaknesses that affect not just public debt management but other core government functions as well.

Indeed, in a number of countries the pilot program work formed the basis for follow-up work under a broader reform agenda, whether as part of World Bank projects or programs or those managed by other donors. For example, in Indonesia, the completion of the diagnostic report and discussions with the government suggested that follow-up work would fit well within a World Bank Government Financial Management and Revenue Administration Project that aims to strengthen efficiency and integrity in public financial management and resource mobilization, principally through strengthening governance, accountability, and transparency. In Kenya, the pilot project was integrated into the Financial and Legal Sector Technical Assistance Project of the World Bank, in coordination with the Commonwealth Secretariat and the Macroeconomic and Financial Management Institute of Eastern and Southern Africa. In Zambia, the government and the donor group decided early in October 2004 that the diagnostic report and the recommendations therein would become part of the ongoing Public

Expenditure Management and Financial Accountability Reform program.[11] Reforms in Zambia's public debt management were also incorporated into the conditions for a World Bank structural adjustment loan.

Other donors have also joined to support the implementation of reform programs in pilot countries. For example, in Croatia, the European Union (EU) funded the implementation phase of the reform program. In Costa Rica, the Financial Sector Reform and Strengthening Initiative is supporting the implementation phase of the project,[12] and in Lebanon, the work under this program is being followed up by integration within the UNDP-funded project Capacity Development for Fiscal Reform and Management. In all of these cases, the original World Bank staff involved in the diagnostic remain involved in various capacities to support the reforms. In Bulgaria, implementation of the pilot program was integrated into an EU project entitled Support for the Implementation of the Medium-Term Strategy and Restructuring of the Ministry of Finance. The project covers budget execution, creation of a treasury single account system, and the implementation of a new financial management information system.[13]

In countries with no immediate prospects for incorporating debt management and debt market development into broader reform programs, the benefits of proceeding in isolation need to be assessed. The chances of success are higher in countries with strong institutions and where the required improvements are more technical. In Tunisia, for example, both the ministry of finance and the central bank have experienced staff and effective governance arrangements, and capacity is being built with the assistance of grants targeted at risk management and specific improvements to information technology systems. As noted earlier, one of the reasons that the reforms in Sri Lanka to shift public debt management out of the central bank did not proceed beyond the planning stage was the limited capacity of the finance ministry. A more effective approach might have been to incorporate public debt management into a broader capacity-building program for the ministry, spanning all of its major functions.[14]

IMPLICATIONS FOR PROVIDERS OF ASSISTANCE

Given the pilot-program experience, how can the World Bank and other providers of assistance best help countries build capacity and implement public debt management reforms? Several observations have emerged from engagements with the countries:

▨ Public debt management, and to a lesser extent domestic government debt market development, does not fit neatly into traditional sectoral categories.[15] Thus, diagnostics with a principal focus on the financial sector, such as the Financial Sector Assessment Program, examine debt management from the perspective of vulnerability of the financial sector and might not address governance or public expenditure management. Debt management as enveloped in assessments with a focus on public expenditure management mainly focuses on debt management systems. Analytical work on macroeconomics approaches debt management from the point of view of its contribution to stabilizing public finances or aiding monetary policy implementation, but it may not address governance and financial market issues.

▨ Diagnostics or assessment reports should be followed up by helping countries initiate reform. The World Bank and other donors can help build a consensus for reform by working with relevant stakeholders as outside experts. Such help can include assisting the dissemination process, promoting discussion, and even brokering between parties, to move toward an agreed strategy for reforms.

▨ Because of the long-term nature of these reforms, donors will be most effective if they are able to stay involved in the process continuously, rather than through one-off engagements. The relationships built between the authorities and the individuals involved in providing advice are important, as is the depth of knowledge that these individuals develop about the country and the reform program. Engaging expertise for specific components is still feasible, but having a source of advice the authorities can count on to maintain a coherent program consistent with the original vision can prove crucial.

▨ As with any project or program, donor coordination must occur to ensure that all components are covered, but not duplicated. Ideally, the authorities in the country should direct this process, but experience in some of the pilot-program countries showed that this is not always possible. Related to the third point above, a coordinating donor can help facilitate the provision of inputs from other providers, based on comparative expertise, availability of funding, and modality for assistance (for example, use of resident advisors, provision of grants or loans, and technical advice missions).

FUTURE WORK

The implementation of the reforms is at a comparatively early stage in some pilot countries and barely beginning in others. To continue to support these efforts, and to build knowledge about the relative effectiveness of the various approaches being implemented, future activities are planned. The first is to develop more-effective indicators of performance for public debt management to permit an assessment of progress over the medium term.[16] Second, efforts will continue to help countries obtain the required expertise and financing to implement reforms. Finally, a follow-up study may be commissioned in a few years to examine the progress of the pilot countries and to obtain a better understanding of the factors underpinning their experiences.

Debt Management Strategy and Risk Management

An explicit public debt management strategy sets out a medium-term framework for how the government will manage the composition of debt.

In developing a debt management strategy, the priority that risk reduction should have over cost savings must be clarified. Avoiding debt default should be the top priority, given the magnitude of the potential output losses and human cost that can accompany default. Some financial crises and sovereign defaults have been precipitated partly because governments have focused on expected cost savings in the short run (for example, by issuing large volumes of short-term debt or debt in foreign currency). This left government finances seriously exposed to changing market conditions and contagion.

A framework should be developed to enable debt managers to identify and manage the trade-offs between expected cost and risk in the government debt portfolio. This framework must be supported by a quantification of risk, including stress tests of the debt portfolio based on the economic and financial shocks to which the country is potentially exposed. Such a framework is the cornerstone of the debt management strategy approved by the finance minister (or ministers acting collectively).

The strategy should also be consistent with, and take into account, the constraints imposed by the macroeconomic framework. Such constraints might limit the composition of the debt portfolios of developing and emerging-market countries more than those in open, developed economies. The constraints could include capital controls, implementation of monetary policy through direct instruments, and a weak fiscal position (the issue of coordination between fiscal and monetary policy and debt management is explored in detail in chapter 4). An underdeveloped domestic government debt market also places constraints on a debt management strategy; *Developing the Domestic Government Debt Market* describes the many facets in this area. Given the complexity and interactions between these considerations, developing a debt management strategy is an iterative process (figure 3.1).

Strategies can be embodied in a benchmark—a quantification of the approved strategy that typically comprises targets for the key risk characteristics of the debt portfolio. These risk characteristics could include limits on debt maturing in a fiscal year, the share of fixed versus floating-rate debt, the share of domestic versus foreign-currency debt, or the currency composition of foreign-currency debt. For countries with less developed markets and considerable uncertainty about access over time, more general guidelines may be more appropriate.

To support the provision of a benchmark or guidelines, a strategy document should outline the supporting analysis and rationale and make clear the nature of the judgments being made (box 3.1).

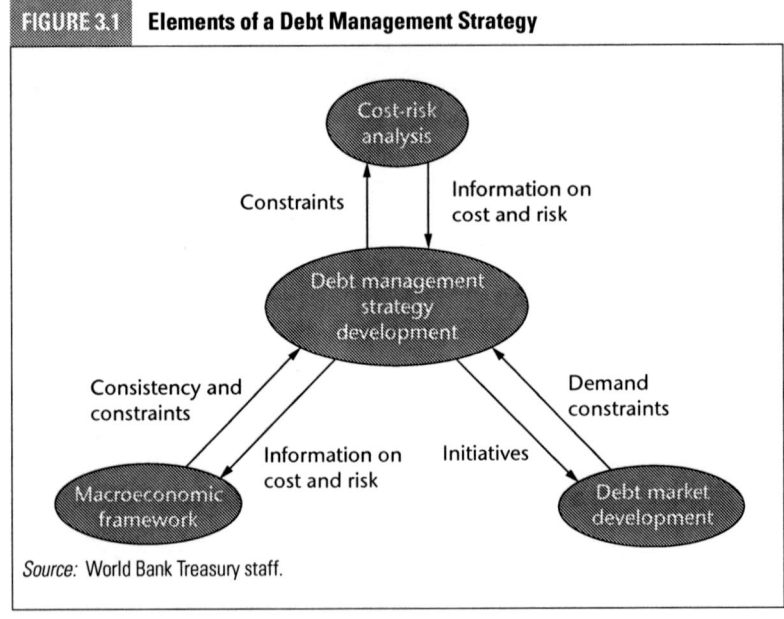

FIGURE 3.1 Elements of a Debt Management Strategy

Source: World Bank Treasury staff.

BOX 3.1 Elements of a Debt Management Strategy

A country's debt management strategy should be drafted in a manner that can be understood by decision makers. Ideally, it should

- describe the risks being managed (currency, interest-rate, refinancing, and credit risks). Examples could be used to indicate how these risks could affect the debt burden.
- provide the historical context for the debt portfolio, including describing changes in the portfolio's size (both absolute and relative to GDP) and composition through time. Changes in relevant market variables should be incorporated, along with commentary on the key events in the evolution of the debt.
- describe the environment for debt management in the future, including fiscal and debt projections, assumptions about exchange and interest rates, and constraints on portfolio choice, especially those relating to market development and the implementation of monetary policy.
- describe the analysis undertaken to support the recommended debt management strategy, clarifying the assumptions used and the limitations of the analysis.
- set out the recommended strategy and its rationale. The explanation should specify ranges for the key risk indicators of the portfolio and the financing program, but could be as detailed as a benchmark portfolio. The strategy should also describe measures or projects that are planned to manage unquantifiable risks and that support debt market development.

While the strategy should be specified for the medium to long term, it should be reviewed periodically to assess whether the assumptions still hold in light of changed circumstances. Such a review should be undertaken annually as part of the budget process, and if the existing strategy is viewed as appropriate, the rationale for its continuation should be stated.

Source: World Bank Treasury staff.

DIAGNOSTICS IN PILOT COUNTRIES

The composition of public debt, and thus the risks to which the governments were exposed, varied considerably across the 12 countries in the pilot program. Such risk indicators, as well as the government's ability to manage these risks, should be viewed within the context of individual country circumstances, including macroeconomic vulnerability, policy coordination, governance arrangements, and capacity.[1] (Table 3.1 shows the main characteristics of the debt portfolios of the pilot countries, summarized by currency and interest rate composition, as well as the maturity profile at the time of the diagnostic reports.)

As table 3.1 shows, at the time of the diagnostics, external debt as a share of total debt was highest in Bulgaria and Zambia, at 88 percent and 85 percent, respectively, while in the other pilot countries, it ranged between 36 percent (Costa Rica) and 68 percent (Nicaragua). While some caution is needed in interpreting the data because of the basis on which it was compiled, on average the countries had significant exposure to currency risk.[2] This is particularly true for those that also had high public debt levels, such as Lebanon and Zambia, where foreign-currency debt amounted to 80 percent and 160 percent of GDP, respectively, representing a significant risk to the governments' finances. However, in most pilot countries, the nature of the external debt provided an opportunity to reduce rollover and interest-rate risks because it tended to be long term and contracted with fixed interest rates. A further consideration when interpreting currency risk is the source of external debt. Kenya, Nicaragua, Pakistan, Sri Lanka, and Zambia obtained funding mainly from multilateral and bilateral concessionary sources at very low cost relative to market borrowing in foreign currencies. Croatia borrowed mainly from the international capital markets, while Bulgaria, Colombia, Costa Rica, Indonesia, Lebanon, and Tunisia used both market and official (multilateral and bilateral) sources.

The composition of the domestic debt portfolio varied, reflecting the differing degrees of development of the domestic government debt markets. Costa Rica, Kenya, Lebanon, Sri Lanka, Tunisia, and Zambia had a high concentration of short-term debt, and Bulgaria, Colombia, Croatia, Indonesia, Nicaragua, and Pakistan achieved some lengthening of the maturity profile. As for the sources of domestic debt, Bulgaria borrowed exclusively through competitive auction systems, while Colombia, Costa Rica, Croatia, Kenya, Pakistan, and Sri Lanka relied on a combination of forced placements with public sector enterprises and banks, and market placements.[3]

At the diagnostic phase, none of the pilot countries had a medium-term, comprehensive debt management strategy based on a systematic analysis of cost and risk, and agreed on at the ministerial level. Colombia had an explicit strategy for external debt only, and Tunisia had targets for the composition of its foreign-currency debt portfolio.

The public debt managers in most pilot countries, however, had a good understanding of the key risks of their debt portfolios, which shaped the way government borrowing was managed. Management actions included measures to reduce the share of external debt in total debt, smoothing the redemption profile, and developing the domestic government debt market. For example, Indonesia, Kenya, Lebanon, and

TABLE 3.1 Debt Composition in the 12 Pilot-Program Countries

Country	Date	Gross public debt to GDP ratio (%)	External to domestic debt ratio	Main characteristics of external debt	Main source of external debt	Main characteristics of domestic debt	Main source of domestic debt
Bulgaria	2002	56.0	88:12	54% US dollars and 30% euro 63% floating rate	30% Brady bonds, 30% from market 40% loans from multilateral and bilateral creditors	70% fixed rate 70% in local currency, 18% US dollar, 12% euro less than 5% of outstanding maturing within next 12 months	Tradable[a]
Colombia	2002	51.0[b]	54:46	83% US dollars, 13% euro, 4% yen 65% fixed rate	62% from market 30% from multilateral and bilateral creditors	38% fixed rate 95% local currency 19% inflation index 16% of outstanding maturing in the next 12 months	80% is TES, of which half placed in the market, half through forced placement with the public sector
Costa Rica	2003	60.0	35:65[c]	73% with maturity of six years and greater (central government debt)	Mostly Eurobonds (69%) followed by multilaterals (21%)	Government debt: 32% maturing in next 12 months; 45% indexed to US dollar Central bank debt: very short term, half issued in US dollars	Public sector banks hold 26%, and other public sector additional 7% Private sector non-financial 23%
Croatia	2004	41.7	60:40[d]	Fixed rate, mainly euro (60%)	Mainly private creditors and institutional investors[e]	58% payable in Croatian kuna but indexed to the euro 60% fixed rate	Domestic banks and non-bank financial institutions

(continued)

TABLE 3.1 *continued*

Country	Date	Gross public debt to GDP ratio (%)	External to domestic debt ratio	Main characteristics of external debt	Main source of external debt	Main characteristics of domestic debt	Main source of domestic debt
Indonesia	2004	73.0	50:50	Long term 69% fixed rate 44% yen, 28% US dollar Concessionary	96% from multilateral and bilateral creditors[f]	65% fixed rate long term fixed up to 15 years	60% tradable debt (recap bonds) of which 72% held by domestic banks and 40% nontradable[g]
Kenya	2002/ 2003	65.0	56:44	Long term and Concessionary	60% multilateral creditors 33% bilateral creditors	70% of outstanding domestic debt has interest rate re-set within next 12 months 40% to mature within the next 12 months Average time to maturity is 1.7 years	60% held by domestic banks, 6% by parastatals
Lebanon	2003	175.0[h]	47:53	US dollar fixed	US dollar Eurobonds, purchased mostly by domestic banks	Average time to maturity is 481 days	Domestic banks
Nicaragua	2004[h]	93.0	68:32	Long term and concessionary	96% multilateral and bilateral creditors	Government: Medium term, mostly non-marketable Central bank: short term All domestic debt indexed to US dollar	Domestic retail investors and a small number of banks

Pakistan	2003/2004	69.0	48:52	Long term, fixed, and concessionary with smooth redemption profile / Mostly in US dollar, yen, and euro / Duration of about seven years	95% multilateral and bilateral creditors[i]	About half the domestic debt has embedded put options.[j]	Domestic banks and retail investors
Sri Lanka	2002	103.0	44:56	Long term, fixed / 41% SDR, 30% yen / 93% concessionary	50% multilateral creditors / 43% bilateral	27% maturing within next 12 months.	60% placed directly with institutional investors / 18% domestic banks
Tunisia	2003	60.5	65:35	Long term, fixed / 43% in euro, 24% in US dollar, and 26% in yen	1/3 market / 2/3 multilateral and bilateral creditors	45% maturing within next 12 months / 100% fixed rate	2/3 marketable
Zambia	2003	187.0	85:15	Long term, fixed / Concessionary	Multilateral and bilateral creditors	Short term	70% commercial banks, also pension funds and Bank of Zambia

Source: The information contained in the table was collected by World Bank staff, mainly during the assessment stage, the timing of which differed across countries.

Note: SDR = Special Drawing Rights.

a. Some 30 percent of total domestic debt is Deposit Insurance Bonds and securities issued for structural reforms; the rest was issued for budget financing.

b. Net public debt as a percentage of GDP.

c. Both the central bank and finance ministry issue domestic debt. About 71 percent of Costa Rica's central government debt carries floating rates.

d. Because of the domestic debt linked to the euro, the foreign-currency exposure is 85 percent of the total debt (National Bank of Croatia presentation for third quarter of 2005).

e. From National Bank of Croatia presentation for third quarter 2005.

f. In March 2004, a US$1 billion international bond with a 10-year maturity was successfully issued and international bonds have since been issued regularly.

g. Most of the nontradable debt is non-interest-bearing treasury notes held by the Bank Indonesia.

h. Post-HIPC completion point.

i. The government issued a US$500 million Eurobond in February 2004 and a US$600 million Islamic Bond in January 2005.

j. About half the domestic financing in Pakistan is raised through the National Savings Schemes (NSS). The NSS instruments have embedded put options, giving holders the right to redeem them before maturity in exchange for a lower return. These options could increase considerably the government's cost of funding if investors shorten duration when yields on NSS instruments fall below market rates.

Nicaragua identified rollover risk as the most important risk, particularly for the domestic debt portfolio. As a result, these countries were keenly aware of the need to develop domestic government debt markets. Hence, the strategy for domestic borrowing was focused on securing a smooth redemption profile by issuing long-term, fixed-rate bonds, mindful of the risk that government bonds could crowd out the private sector. Colombia and Tunisia identified currency risk as the main concern and their strategies have been to gradually increase the share of domestic-currency debt in their total debt portfolios.

While implicit strategies based on a general understanding of cost-risk trade-offs have largely been reasonable, and have provided some guidance on reducing risk, they are limiting in a number of respects. First, the lack of a thorough analysis has meant that the trade-offs between possible cost outcomes were only partially understood. For example, pilot countries with access to concessionary loans, such as Indonesia, Kenya, Pakistan, Sri Lanka, and Zambia, sought to borrow as much as possible in foreign currency on concessionary terms,[4] and financed the rest through domestic borrowing, taking into account the absorptive capacity of the domestic market. The split between external and domestic debt was a residual outcome, not the result of a conscious strategy.

In practice, the strategy is driven primarily by the volumes and terms offered by official sources and there is little understanding of the possible consequences, for the budget and debt sustainability, of the trade-off between foreign-currency debt (with very low interest rates and long maturities) and domestic debt (typically with shorter maturities and higher interest rates). For example, an after-the-fact analysis of the debt dynamics of Sri Lanka suggested that the increase in outstanding foreign debt of 13 percent between 2001 and 2002 was due mainly to depreciation of the domestic currency. At the same time, domestic interest payments rose by 24 percent over the previous year, or from 6.7 percent to 7.4 percent of GDP, because of the domestic debt portfolio's high interest rate exposure.[5]

Another consequence of the absence of an overall strategy is inconsistency in the management of different parts of the debt portfolio. In some cases, the strategy and actions to reduce risks or costs for one subportfolio conflicted with those of another.[6] For example, in Indonesia managers of part of the foreign-currency debt aimed to increase the share of floating-rate debt, while those responsible for another subportfolio aimed to do the reverse; the strategy for one subportfolio in Pakistan sought to increase the share of Japanese yen, while another aimed to reduce its share (table 3.2).

TABLE 3.2   Examples of Conflicting Debt Management Strategies for Subportfolios

Country	Unit 1	Unit 2	Other Units
Colombia	Unit responsible for marketable domestic debt was interested in domestic debt market development.	Unit responsible for cash management and for managing unmarketable securities has strategy of forced lending to state entities.	n.a.
Costa Rica	To keep debt servicing cost low, unit responsible for debt and cash management wished to continue with direct placement of debt with public sector entities.	Unit concerned with high cost of quasi-fiscal deficit and the credibility threat of weakening the central bank balance sheet saw as priority reducing the cost of debt by issuing foreign-currency debt.	Unit concerned with improving effectiveness of open market operations was interested in development of the domestic debt market, willing to pay higher price.
Indonesia	Unit managing the securities market subportfolio identified reducing interest-rate risk as a priority, and aimed to increase the share of fixed-rate debt.	Unit responsible for managing bilateral and multilateral loans saw it had too much fixed-rate debt, therefore its strategy was to increase floating-rate debt.	n.a.
Pakistan	Unit responsible for economic analysis decided to borrow as much as possible in Japanese yen because of low financing cost.	Unit responsible for developing the debt management strategy suggests priority was to reduce exposure to Japanese yen because they believed that the portfolio was overexposed to this currency.	n.a.

Source: World Bank Treasury staff.
Note: n.a. = Not applicable.

Finally, the absence of an explicit strategy agreed on at a high level means that choices about borrowing might be inconsistent through time. An informal strategy is neither binding nor transparent and may allow short-term expediency to dominate (to reduce budgetary costs) the medium-term goal of prudent risk management. It can also result in the priorities of monetary policy implementation being too readily accepted.

(This issue is discussed in chapter 4.) In other cases, the absence of an explicit strategy has resulted in ambiguity about how to resolve policy differences between different parts of government.[7]

Some countries had already recognized the need for better information on cost and risk trade-offs and were making advances at the time of the diagnostic. Costa Rica, Indonesia, Lebanon, Nicaragua, and Sri Lanka had begun analyzing costs and risks in their debt portfolios, while Bulgaria and Colombia had been moving ahead with such analysis for some time. In Nicaragua and Zambia, the analysis was limited to the domestic debt portfolio and to generating the maturity profile for measuring and managing refinancing risk, which was their primary concern. In Sri Lanka, the time horizon of the analysis of sensitivities to domestic interest rates extended only to one year. The latter three countries, however, were at the initial stages of their projects.

In some pilot countries, officials had conducted other research relevant to developing a debt management strategy. Colombia had begun researching the financial characteristics of the main assets of the government, namely, tax revenues. In Tunisia, the central bank had developed a framework for the currency composition of external debt, basing it on the currency basket targeted for the Tunisian dinar, which, in turn, was based on the composition of current account flows. Such an analysis is useful for an economy with a closed capital account under a managed exchange rate regime.

ACTION PLANS AND REFORM EXPERIENCES

The 12 pilot-program countries have progressed, to varying degrees, in taking measures to improve the analysis of cost and risk, to develop comprehensive and formal debt management strategies, and to reduce risk. These are reviewed in turn.

The Analysis of Cost and Risk

As a first step in improving the analysis of cost and risk, pilot countries have identified and described existing risks in the total debt portfolio. A number of countries (Colombia, Indonesia, Sri Lanka, and Tunisia) have published descriptions of the composition of the total debt by domestic and foreign currencies, interest rate structures, and maturity profile; Bulgaria publishes this information in a monthly bulletin. Costa Rica has been providing this information for all public debt excluding that issued by the central bank, which will be added as a next step. Lebanese authorities plan to produce a full set of risk indicators for the public debt, to supplement reporting on composition by currency. A prerequisite for producing information on debt composition and risk indicators is the maintenance of reliable debt recording systems; clearly, countries without such systems need to remedy this first (Kenya, Pakistan, and Zambia).

The next step in analyzing cost and risk is to define a base case and alternative strategies and compare these under a variety of market scenarios (differing exchange rates and interest rates). This has been a significant challenge for the pilot countries because of the technical skills it requires, but Bulgaria, Colombia, and Indonesia have been building capacity in the area, with Indonesia starting to apply this analysis for the total debt portfolio. In Costa Rica, Sri Lanka, and Tunisia, cost-risk analysis has been planned with assistance funded by various grants and donors. The emphasis in all of these countries was to begin the process with scenario analysis to develop familiarity with the underlying risks and to quickly obtain a more quantitative understanding of the nature of the trade-offs that decision makers must make. After this, more advanced stochastic simulation can be developed, depending on the need for more detailed information in specific countries.

In conducting the scenario analysis, a clear understanding of the constraints that can bind portfolio choices is crucial. Work planned in Costa Rica included an analysis of the historical evolution of the debt composition, to better understand the extent to which weak macroeconomic fundamentals and limitations in the domestic debt market have restricted the borrowing options available to the debt manager and shaped the management of public debt in the past. Chapter 4 provides examples of the impact of these interactions on the development of a debt management strategy. (See also *Developing the Domestic Government Debt Market*.)

Developing Comprehensive Debt Management Strategies

Measures to develop comprehensive and formal debt management strategies involved codifying existing practices and developing guidelines approved by the highest authority responsible for managing the debt, usually the minister of finance or the council of ministers.

Bulgaria, Colombia, and Indonesia produced debt management strategy documents during the course of the pilot program. Indonesia's debt management strategy document was approved by the minister of finance and presented to parliament in September 2005. The document describes the existing risks in the debt portfolio, options and constraints, and the rationale for choices made in the borrowing program. It then outlines the general debt management strategy for 2005–09 (box 3.2). The document also codifies existing practices for making borrowing decisions. Although nothing new for the Indonesian government, codification of existing practices reduces the risk of inconsistent implementation of the borrowing program over time. The next planned step is to incorporate results from more rigorous, forward-looking analysis of cost and risk and strengthen the information base for decision making.

The Bulgarian strategy document, first published in 2003 and again in 2006, summarizes the country's debt management policy for the next three years, pursuant to the Government Debt Law. The document describes the institutional structure, the regulatory arrangements, and the current composition of the debt. It also reviews the risks arising from the size and structure of the debt and defines the objectives for its management. Specific measures for achieving these goals are defined, and are consistent with the three-year macroeconomic forecasts and analysis of different scenarios for the domestic and international market environment. More precise strategic targets are also established (table 3.3). The ranges allow for some variation in the targets from interest rate and exchange rate movements.[8]

The strategy is updated annually in accordance with economic outcomes and portfolio results, and approved by the council of ministers at the same time as the rolling three-year budget forecast.

Colombia's Higher Council of Fiscal Policy, with input from the finance ministry's Public Debt Directorate, has also produced a debt management strategy.[9] It describes the debt management goals and general strategy, and gives priority to diversifying funding sources and reducing foreign-currency and refinancing risks. The strategy also establishes strategic targets for total debt. It describes the debt management operations carried out during the year and discusses the council's achievements.

TABLE 3.3   Bulgaria's Strategic Targets, 2003–06

Indicator	Strategic target	Ranges
Ratio of fixed to floating debt	50:50	+/− 10%
Ratio of external to domestic debt	80:20	—
Ratio of US dollar to euro debt	30:70	+/− 5%
Duration	5.25 years	+/− 0.25%

Source: Bulgaria Ministry of Finance 2003.
Note: — = Not available.

BOX 3.2   **Indonesia's General Strategy in State Debt Management for 2005–09**

To achieve the goals of long-term state debt management to minimize debt costs at a controlled risk level, the government's medium-term general strategy for the years 2005–9 is as follows:

Reduction of state debts. To reduce fiscal sustainability risks, efforts are necessary to reduce debt stocks maturing in 2005–09. Cash buyback or debt switching will be used. If the finance situation allows, settlement of state debts before maturity is a priority for debts that could raise exposure to risks in the state debt portfolio.

Simplification of state debt portfolio. To facilitate risk management, comprehensive management of debts should be conducted to simplify the variety of debt instruments in the state debt portfolio structure, thereby allowing more efficient management.

Issuance and procurement of state debt in the rupiah. To reduce exchange-rate risk, priority will be given to issuing new state debt in the Indonesian rupiah, and a gradual and planned reduction of foreign-currency loans will be attempted. The use of a hedging instrument available in the market, such as a currency swap, will also be considered.

Minimizing refinancing risks. To manage the refinancing risks during 2006–09, the issuance of medium-term to long-term state bonds will be prioritized to maintain the average duration of the domestic securities portfolio at four years.

Cash management bills will be issued only to cover short-term cash necessity (cash mismatch) and not to cover the deficit or the refinancing of maturing state bonds.

The debt buyback program consists of buying back debt in cash (cash buyback) or exchanging it for debt that matures during 2006–09 (debt switching). Buyback, in addition to reducing the refinancing risks over the period, is also intended to maintain the stability of the debt market price when the market is bearish. Buyback and debt switching can be implemented simultaneously to improve market liquidity by pulling out the nonliquid series (off-the-run-bonds) and replacing them with liquid benchmark issues.

To reduce refinancing risks in the offshore loan portfolio, the authorities might consider using the debt rescheduling facility provided by creditors for the soft and semi-commercial loans, while still paying attention to the risk factors and reducing state debt expenses.

Improvement in the portion of state debt with fixed interest rates. Attempts will be made to acquire new debt with fixed interest rates, to avoid additional expenses that must be paid by the government that might arise from the increase in the interest rate in the market if debts with floating interest rates have been acquired. The target is to balance fixed-interest-rate and floating-interest-rate debt at 50:50. This strategy also helps provide certainty to the government in calculating the amount of the interest costs that will become expenditures in a one-year budget. Additionally, fixed-interest debt can help market liquidity because it can facilitate the establishment of a benchmark yield curve in the secondary market. Interest-rate risk can also be reduced by using the interest rate swap facility provided in the financial market.

Reduction of export credit portion. Soft loans, with low interest rates and for long terms, should be given priority over commercial loans, particularly export credit.

Source: Unofficial translation of "Strategy on State Debt Management of the Republic of Indonesia: 2005–2009," Department of Finance of the Republic of Indonesia, Jakarta, September 2005.

To facilitate the implementation of the strategy, Colombia has established an annual directive. For example, the 2005 directive for external capital market operations was to continue the pre-financing operations executed in 2004 and pre-finance all financing needs for 2006. The directive for domestic debt market operations was to obtain a specific amount of funding from the domestic debt market by issuing Treasury securities; strengthen the liquidity of short-maturity securities, promoting the development of the short end of the yield curve; reduce debt service through debt management operations, freeing up short-term cash flow; and develop and deepen the liquidity of all points on the yield curve by reopening issues and developing instruments of longer maturity that facilitate more efficient pricing, diminish issuance costs, and provide the market with a zero-risk reference.

When governments do not have sufficient information to establish targets or benchmarks for the portfolio, establishing a general strategy or directives can be a useful first step. Even for countries facing significant constraints on financing choices, a strategy can provide a framework to ensure borrowing is undertaken in a manner consistent with debt sustainability (for example, setting minimum levels of concessionality and controlling the concentration of maturities).

Reducing Risks

Many of the pilot-program countries gave priority to reducing currency risk and have managed in recent years to boost the relative share of domestic debt (Bulgaria, Colombia, Costa Rica, Kenya, Nicaragua, Pakistan, and Zambia). In Croatia, Indonesia, and Lebanon, the ratio changed little, while in Sri Lanka and Tunisia, the share of domestic debt as a share of total debt declined over the short period analyzed (table 3.4).[10]

Although increasing the share of domestic-currency debt has helped reduce these countries' portfolios' exposure to currency movements, domestic debt has tended to be short-term, thereby increasing interest-rate and rollover risks. The Indonesian and Nicaraguan authorities have been working to smooth the redemption profile of the domestic debt portfolio through debt buybacks and renegotiations with private sector lenders.[11] In Colombia, inflation-indexed instruments played a critical role in extending domestic maturities; Colombia has also been successful in issuing longer-dated, fixed-rate securities (Colombia issued 15-year debt, the longest tenor ever to be placed in the domestic market).[12] Bulgaria has been able to extend the yield curve as a result of increased demand for longer-dated securities, following stabilization of the macro-

TABLE 3.4 Changes in the Composition of External and Domestic Debt of Pilot-Program Countries (as percentage of total debt and of GDP)

Country	Domestic debt (% total debt)		Domestic debt (% GDP)		Total debt (% GDP)	
	(Date 1)	*(Date 2)*	*(Date 1)*	*(Date 2)*	*(Date 1)*	*(Date 2)*
Bulgaria	9.0 (2000)	18.0 (2004)	6.9 (2000)	7.0 (2004)	80.6 (2000)	40.0 (2004)
Colombia	59.0 (2002)	66.0 (2004)	41.0 (2002)	38.5 (2004)	69.0 (2002)	58.5 (2004)
Costa Rica	58.0 (2000)	61.0 (2004)	26.8 (2000)	33.0 (2004)	46.5 (2000)	54.0 (2004)
Croatia	41.0 (2002)	42.0 (2004)	21.0 (2002)	22.5 (2004)	50.5 (2002)	53.0 (2004)
Indonesia	48.0 (2001)	50.0 (2004)	44.0 (2001)	27.0 (2004)	92.0 (2001)	54.0 (2004)
Lebanon	55.0 (2002)	49.0 (2004)	97.0 (2002)	96.8 (2004)	177.7 (2002)	179.0 (2004)
Kenya	29.0 (2001)	42.0 (2004)	33.0 (1997–8)	42.0 (2004–5)	114.0 (2001)	100.0 (2004)
Nicaragua	37.0 (2001)	31.0 (2004)	103.0 (2001)	30.0 (2004)	276.0 (2001)	93.0 (2004)
Pakistan	49.0 (2000–1)	53.0 (2003–4)	43.3 (2000–1)	36.3 (2003–4)	88.8 (2000–1)	68.0 (2003–4)
Sri Lanka	56.0 (2000)	53.0 (2004)	53.8 (2000)	56.4 (2004)	96.8 (2000)	105.5 (2004)
Tunisia	40.0 (2000)	35.0 (2003)	24.3 (2000)	21.0 (2002)	61.4 (2000)	60.0 (2003)
Zambia	4.0 (1999)	11.0 (2003)	7.7 (2000)	21.0 (2003)	218.0 (1999)	195.0 (2003)

Sources: Bulgaria Ministry of Finance 2005; Croatia Ministry of Finance 2005; Indonesia Ministry of Finance 2005; Central Bank of Kenya 2001, 2005; Nicaragua Ministry of Finance n.d.; World Bank Treasury staff; IMF 2006c.

economic environment and the banking system, the entry of pension funds with long-term capital, and improved confidence by external and domestic investors in the government's policies, including debt management.[13] In Croatia, instruments payable in local currency but indexed to the euro were issued to extend the maturity profile; there were also two issuances of long-term kuna-denominated bonds. Lebanon has managed to reduce the high refinancing risk that characterized the domestic debt portfolio by gradually issuing longer-dated domestic-currency debt, with the issuance of three- and five-year debt beginning in 2003.[14] Zambia has also achieved some lengthening of the domestic debt maturity profile by introducing three- and five-year debt during the second half of 2005.

The Kenyan and Sri Lankan governments have managed to extend domestic maturities rather rapidly, although partly because of forced placement with public sector entities or direct placement with domestic banks. But significant refinancing risk remains in Kenya, because 75 percent of the outstanding domestic debt falls due within the next 24 months. In Tunisia, the controlled interest rate environment has allowed investors to buy long-term, fixed-rate paper even when their own liabilities have been mainly short-term. This has created demand for longer-dated paper that might not have arisen had there been no interest rate controls.

The Indonesian authorities are aware that government borrowing can crowd out private investment and have therefore limited growth in domestic borrowing. The macroeconomic program agreed on by the Zambian authorities with the International Monetary Fund also aimed at containing domestic borrowing to avoid crowding out resources available to the private sector. As a result, domestic debt declined from 22 percent of GDP in 2003 to an estimated 16.5 percent at the end of 2005.

Bulgaria, Colombia, and Tunisia have used currency- and interest-rate swap transactions to transform the existing composition of their debt portfolios toward the desired structure. Bulgaria has transformed its World Bank loans from US dollars to euro and from floating-rate to fixed-rate exposure; Colombia has carried out numerous swap transactions transforming its foreign-currency exposure as well into domestic-currency exposure, and from floating to fixed interest rates; and Tunisia has transformed its World Bank loans with floating-rate exposures into fixed-rate.

CONCLUSIONS AND INSIGHTS

The experience of the 12 pilot countries shows a broadly based understanding of the risks in public debt portfolios, as well as some actions taken to mitigate these risks. Still, moving from a series of informal decisions to a formal strategy—agreed on at the ministerial level—was seen as important by some governments because of the pressures to resort to expedient measures to cut costs over the short run, at the expense of greater long-run risk.

A formal debt management strategy can be implemented gradually, with quality improvements over time as capacity is strengthened and more analysis is undertaken. A useful first step is to codify and document the rationale and existing processes that define the composition of the debt. This allows multiple players to see the overall picture. It also clarifies the constraints imposed by access to funding (including domestic government debt market development) and macroeconomic management and provides a reference point for further analysis.

Relatively simple analysis is often a sufficient basis upon which to build a strategy, particularly when a country's portfolio contains significant financial risk or market access is constrained (or both). In these circumstances, the direction in which the debt portfolio should move is relatively clear and will frequently be determined by what is possible given the constraints. Nevertheless, even an elementary quantification of risk can help decision makers better understand the trade-offs they are making and help them determine the desired currency composition on their own rather than having it set by the donor community. As decisions about the composition of the debt become more nuanced—once major risks to the government's financial position have been addressed—more sophisticated analysis is required.

Specification of a debt management strategy can range from simply having an intended direction for the portfolio to specific targets or a borrowing program, usually expressed with ranges. For countries with severely constrained funding choices, especially those limited to highly concessional borrowing (where terms are dictated by the creditor) and with limited domestic markets, a more general specification usually makes more sense. For some risks, however (rollover risk in the domestic-currency portfolio, for example), "sharper" targets might be preferable. In all cases, the debt management strategy should spell out the nature of the constraints and provide a rationale for the chosen approach.

Coordination between Debt Management, Fiscal Policy, Monetary Policy, and Cash Management

ebt managers, fiscal policy advisors, and central bankers should all understand the objectives of debt management and fiscal and monetary policies, given the interdependencies between their different policy instruments.

Although the government's fiscal advisors are usually responsible for carrying out debt sustainability analysis, information on the financial risks arising from the debt portfolio and debt servicing projections provided by debt managers are a key input—especially in countries with high debt levels. A forward-looking debt management strategy that includes a range of financial market scenarios provides useful insights into the impact of changes in debt servicing costs on fiscal sustainability. The output of such an analysis can be the basis for policy coordination to ensure that the policy mix is consistent and sustainable. Debt managers should ensure that appropriate communications channels are in place to inform the government in a timely way of any emerging debt sustainability problems.

Where the level of financial development allows, countries should separate debt management and monetary policy objectives and accountability.

Effective cash management contributes to efficient debt management and assists in the implementation of fiscal and monetary policies. The government debt manager requires assurance that sufficient cash is available to meet debt obligations as they fall due. Attempting to meet this basic requirement when cash management practices are inadequate can result in large idle balances and over-borrowing, with associated negative fiscal consequences. The central bank requires accurate government cash forecasts to manage banking system liquidity efficiently.

DIAGNOSTICS IN PILOT COUNTRIES

Coordinating Debt Management and Fiscal Policy and the Budget Process

Most pilot-program countries had high debt levels coupled with heavy interest burdens that contributed to the overall budget deficit at the time of the diagnostics. An indicator of the interest burden is the share of interest costs in total revenue, or as a share of GDP. Lebanon had the highest as a share of total revenue, at 61 percent, followed by Sri Lanka, with 45 percent (table 4.1). The low interest-to-revenue and to-GDP ratios, despite high debt levels, for countries such as Kenya, Nicaragua, and Zambia might be explained by the relative importance of external loans in total debt and the extent of their concessionality.

Because of high debt levels, and the desire to stabilize or lower the debt burden, the governments of Bulgaria, Colombia, Costa Rica, Indonesia, Lebanon, and Pakistan have run tight fiscal policies and recorded positive primary balances, while most of the others have been reducing the primary gap. Such efforts could be jeopardized, however, if interest payments rise suddenly. A key consideration in supporting these countries' fiscal efforts was thus to minimize the variability of debt servicing costs in the budget and the impact on fiscal sustainability.

While fiscal policy should ideally be formulated for a medium- to long-term horizon, in reality it was driven by annual budget cycles in most pilot-program countries. Several pilot governments became myopic when managing budget outcomes over the short run (Costa Rica, Lebanon, Pakistan, and Sri Lanka), resulting in pressure on debt managers to cut costs in the current budget period, at the expense of increasing risk over the medium term. The lack of a formal debt management strategy in these pilot countries facilitated the dominance of such short-term pressures and allowed the risk profile of the debt portfolio to deteriorate.

For example, in Costa Rica during 1999–2004, the riskiness of the maturity structure and currency composition increased; at the same time, reliance on short-term debt and the use of foreign-currency debt in the domestic market intensified, in an effort to limit financing costs. In Lebanon, following the accumulation of debt during the reconstruction period, the fiscal authorities changed course and generated primary surpluses. But controlling debt servicing costs was considered key to stabi-

TABLE 4.1   Debt Levels and Debt Burdens in Pilot-Program Countries

Country	Date	Public debt to GDP (%)	Budget deficit to GDP (%)	Primary balance to GDP (%)	Interest payments to GDP (%)	Interest payments to total revenue (%)
Bulgaria	2002	56.0	0.6	1.6	2.3	5.6
Colombia	2002	55.7	3.6	0.9	4.0	26.0
Costa Rica	2003	54.5	2.9	0.3	4.3	32.0[a]
Croatia	2003	41.7	6.2	−2.3	2.1	5.0
Indonesia	2004	54.0	1.2	2.1	2.8	18.7
Kenya[b]	2002/03	65.0	3.7	−0.49	2.7	11.0
Lebanon	2003	175.0	14.6	3.6	18.0	61.0
Nicaragua[c]	2004	93.0	6.3	−3.2	2.7	11.9
Pakistan	2003/04	69.0	2.4	1.8	3.5	23.8
Sri Lanka	2002	103.0	8.9	−1.6	7.4	44.6
Tunisia	2003	60.5	3.2	−0.4	2.8	12.0
Zambia	2003	187.0	6.6	−2.1	5.8	15.0

Sources: Central Bank of Sri Lanka 2003; IMF 2003, 2004a, 2004c, 2004d, 2005b, 2005c, 2006c; Bulgaria 2003; Nicaragua n. d.; Colombia Ministry of Finance and Public Credit, n. d.; World Bank 2004b.
a. Interest payments correspond to central government debt.
b. Fiscal year runs from July to June.
c. Nicaragua's public sector deficit as a percentage of GDP before grants.

lizing the debt level. This, combined with high levels of dollarization, forced Lebanon's debt management authorities to contract more foreign-currency debt relative to domestic debt to finance the budget deficit. In Sri Lanka, weak fiscal performance resulted in a large and rapid accumulation of debt, which led to the adoption of a borrowing strategy in 2000 and 2001 in which domestic securities were issued mainly in the shorter end of the market. Combined with high borrowing requirements and high interest rates, the strategy contributed to a 59 percent increase in total debt servicing cost between 2001 and 2002.[1]

Recognizing the risks of setting fiscal policy in a short time frame, some pilot countries used medium-term planning. The budget projections in Bulgaria, Colombia, Croatia, Kenya, and Nicaragua used a three-year rolling basis and Tunisia's was determined within the framework of a five-year plan. This helped debt managers focus on the medium term in developing their borrowing plans. Pakistan and Sri Lanka have enacted fiscal responsibility legislation and plan to begin multiyear budgeting.

Coordination at the operational level is vital for ensuring that debt service forecasts are incorporated into the budget preparation process and that debt managers receive information on forecasted budget deficits as input to their projections. Colombia, Indonesia, Sri Lanka, and Tunisia enjoyed clear separation of responsibilities as well as effective sharing of inputs. In addition, the authorities in these countries used a common set of macroeconomic, interest rate, and exchange rate assumptions for their respective forecasts.

Close coordination between the debt management and fiscal policy units in the ministry of finance is particularly important in countries with debt sustainability concerns, because the choice of funding sources and terms can have a significant impact on fiscal outcomes. In Kenya, Nicaragua, Sri Lanka, and Zambia, priority was placed on maximizing borrowing from concessional sources, with the residual to be funded on commercial terms in the domestic market. In reality, however, domestic borrowing grew more rapidly than anticipated when concessional borrowing proved insufficient to finance the budget deficit.

Traditional fiscal sustainability analysis—in which the dynamics of the debt-to-GDP ratio are analyzed based on the composition of existing debt (particularly the currency composition) under different assumptions for economic growth, real interest rates, foreign exchange, and the primary surplus—was carried out at the central banks of Costa Rica,[2] Nicaragua, and Sri Lanka, but with little input and involvement from the fiscal authorities or debt managers.[3] In Colombia, the analysis was coordinated by the fiscal policy unit with the help of the macroeconomic programming unit of the finance ministry, but with little participation from debt managers. At the time of the country diagnostics, none of the pilot countries had conducted fiscal sustainability analysis that included scenarios or simulations with a range of debt portfolios to determine those that reduced the risk of unsustainable outcomes.

Coordinating Debt Management and Monetary Policy

Separating debt management and monetary policy implementation was a challenge for a number of the pilot-program countries, largely for two reasons: First, such separation was not easy when the technical capacity in the finance ministry was weak, often resulting in the central bank assuming responsibility for domestic debt management, as in Kenya, Lebanon, Pakistan, Sri Lanka, and Zambia.[4] In most cases, the central bank acted as an agent for the ministry of finance, but few had a formal agency agreement. With this approach, to ensure separation of policies, the ministry of finance should be responsible for formulating the borrowing strategy and for deciding on auction allocation, including whether and at what levels to set reserve pricing. Given capacity constraints, however, some of the central banks were effectively making the final decisions (table 4.2).

Second, separation of debt management and monetary policy was a challenge where the domestic debt market was underdeveloped and both the ministry of finance and the central bank used short-term government debt as policy instruments (Kenya, Pakistan, and Zambia). Furthermore, in countries where the central bank did not hold sufficient government securities in its portfolio to conduct liquidity management operations in the secondary market—particularly when there was structural excess liquidity in the system—the central banks issued short-dated securities in their own names (Costa Rica, Indonesia, Lebanon, and Nicaragua). The Lebanese central bank also issued longer-term securities in its own name.

The lack of separation between debt management and monetary management highlights the risk of a policy conflict—markets might fear that the central bank is unwilling to raise interest rates to fight inflation because of its desire to keep borrowing costs low.

TABLE 4.2   Central Bank's Decision-Making Authority for Domestic Debt Management

Country	Decision-making authority
Kenya	The central bank proposes to the ministry of finance different options for the yearly strategy in the domestic market. It controls decisions concerning auction results, with very limited input from the ministry in the decision-making process.
Pakistan	The central bank decides the amount to be issued, the maturities, and the cutoff price for treasury bill auctions. For medium- and longer-term bonds, the finance ministry determines the amounts and tenors, but the central bank decides the auction cutoff price.
Sri Lanka	The Monetary Law stipulates that "no new loans shall be raised by the government or by any agency, whether in pursuance of authority conferred by any written law or otherwise, unless the advice of the monetary Board has first been obtained upon the monetary implication of the proposed loan or issue."
Zambia	The Tender Committee decides the total amount of government securities to be issued at auction. The committee consists of the governor and several directors of the central bank, as well as senior management from the ministry of finance (but the latter is, in practice, not represented). The financial markets department of the central bank, in turn, decides the maturity breakdown of the securities to be issued.

Source: World Bank Treasury staff.

This undermining of the credibility of monetary policy is compounded when the central bank has a weak capital position and significant short-term liabilities, which exposes its balance sheet to increases in the same interest rates that it controls through its policy tools.[5] Large quasi-fiscal losses and negative capital positions of the central banks were observed in Costa Rica and Nicaragua, and to a lesser extent in Indonesia.

Poor monetary policy credibility contributes to a high degree of dollarization, as seen in Costa Rica, Lebanon, and Nicaragua, because citizens preferred to hold much of their savings in foreign, rather than domestic, currency. This, in turn, has implications for debt management and domestic government debt market development, because authorities might be unable to issue debt in domestic currency and extend the yield curve beyond shorter maturities.

Colombia's law, however, requires that all central bank open market operations be carried out exclusively with government securities. The central bank in Sri Lanka uses repurchase agreements and reverse repurchase agreement transactions in government securities to implement monetary policy.

Monetary financing of the government deficit was prohibited in most pilot countries. Kenya, Sri Lanka, and Zambia allow some leeway for central bank financing, whereas Pakistan has no legal restriction against it. The scope for monetary financing allows the finance ministry to withdraw from the market completely, or not to accept low bids in auctions. In addition to the impact this has on monetary policy credibility, it also reduces incentives for developing the market and artificially lowers the cost of financing to the government.

In turn, de facto monetary financing of the government, in which the central bank participates directly in the primary market for government debt, was observed in Lebanon and Sri Lanka. In these countries, market participants might fear that such an action constitutes intervention to support prices to limit public debt servicing cost; it might also hinder the development of money and bond markets. The Colombian central bank, though, is prohibited from buying public debt instruments in the primary market.

Coordinating Debt Management and Cash Management

Poor forecasting and management of the government's cash was an issue in many of the pilot countries. In most cases, cash flows relating to debt servicing were forecast well and deficiencies related to other types of expenditure and revenues (Costa Rica, Indonesia, Kenya, Lebanon, Pakistan, Sri Lanka, and Tunisia). This indicated that coordination between debt managers and officials responsible for cash forecasting, typically a budget execution department in the finance ministry, was working well. In Croatia, the budget execution unit produced monthly forecasts but the debt management unit produced quarterly reports. Central banks sometimes played a role, given their interest in the impact of changes in government cash balances on liquidity in the banking system. In Bulgaria, Indonesia, and Sri Lanka, debt managers and the central bank exchanged information at weekly or monthly coordination committees. But Nicaragua and Zambia had problems in forecasting debt servicing and government expenditure and revenues.

Inaccurate forecasting of government cash flows limits the scope for active cash management. One consequence for debt managers is the need to finance short-term cash flow with longer-dated debt (Pakistan, Sri Lanka, Tunisia, and Zambia). Such a lack of decoupling between debt and cash management is expensive and made debt management unpredictable because it did not allow the government to follow an issuance schedule based on a pre-published calendar. In Sri Lanka, the amount of securities issued at each auction was largely determined by a need to issue the same amount of debt that was maturing to avoid cash flow mismatches because the cash manager (the treasury) wished to avoid volatility in daily cash balances arising from domestic debt management activities. In Tunisia, variability in the government's cash flows had a significant impact on the volume of monthly auctions of bonds, which, in turn, created uncertainty for investors and added to the cost of borrowing.

Passive cash management also results in large cash cushions to ensure that money is available for debt service, because the consequences of cash shortfalls can be severe.[6] In Bulgaria, Kenya, and Pakistan, large cash balances were maintained in the central bank's current account. In Sri Lanka, interest is not paid on government deposits with state banks and the central bank. Cash shortfalls were managed by raising short-term funds in the market (Colombia and Croatia), running arrears (Croatia, Sri Lanka, and Zambia), or running overdrafts with the central bank and commercial banks (Sri Lanka). Only Colombia actively managed high cash balances.

The impact of passive cash management on monetary policy implementation and money market development is discussed in *Developing the Domestic Government Debt Market*.

ACTION PLANS AND REFORM EXPERIENCES

Reforms to fiscal and monetary policies were outside the scope of the pilot program, which focused more on policy coordination issues (that is, the implementation of debt management policies that contribute to a consistent overall macroeconomic policy mix and ensure a sustainable level of public debt).

The debt levels of most of the pilot countries were high. To better understand policy priorities, the countries can be divided into two categories: those where the debt dynamics increased public-debt-to-GDP levels at the time of the diagnostic, and those enjoying stable or decreasing debt levels. For the first group (Colombia, Costa Rica,[7] Croatia, Lebanon, and Sri Lanka), the priority was to establish and sustain fiscal discipline.[8] However, prudent debt management was also considered key to supporting the main policy actions, because public finances remained highly vulnerable to shocks. For example, Lebanon articulated a coordinated policy action plan in the Paris II program, which outlined a debt reduction strategy based on the three pillars of a continued increase in the primary surplus, institutional reforms to enhance the credibility of policies, and structural reforms to improve competitiveness and growth.[9] The government also committed itself to refrain from resorting to central bank financing.

In Nicaragua, the goal was to ensure that long-term sustainability was maintained following the attainment of the Heavily Indebted Poor Countries completion point in January 2004.[10] The authorities thus committed themselves to implementing sound fiscal policies and prudent borrowing policies based on highly concessional external funding—which kept new borrowing in line with the expected repayment capacity and reduced domestic debt. This coordinated policy statement was to be formalized in a draft Fiscal Responsibility Act, which did not materialize.

Sri Lanka addressed debt sustainability concerns in two ways: First, it introduced a series of discretionary measures to reduce the primary deficit and improve debt management. Second, the government enacted the Fiscal Management (Responsibility) Act of 2002, which sought to bring more discipline to the fiscal process. A medium-term fiscal sustainability analysis conducted by the central bank demonstrated the need for coordinated policy action. It included maintaining sustained positive primary balances and high economic growth, as well as curbing the rapid rise in expensive domestic market borrowing, to move the debt dynamics onto a downward trajectory. In addition, to enhance policy coordination, Sri Lanka set the improvement of treasury cash management and treasury operations as a goal.

Public sector debt in Costa Rica and Croatia grew substantially up to 2004.[11] Amid sluggish economic growth, the primary surpluses were insufficient to offset a high interest burden, resulting in a rising debt ratio. Fiscal sustainability analysis in both countries showed high sensitivity of the public debt portfolio to movements in interest rates, exchange rates, and output economic growth. To reverse the negative debt dynamics, the authorities agreed to a medium-term fiscal program aimed at expanding the primary surplus of the consolidated public sector and at improving public debt management.

In Colombia, the upward trajectory of debt ratios was reversed starting in 2003, due partly to the recovery of economic growth, the reduction in the primary deficit, and appreciation of the local currency. A new law adopted in 2003 requiring the creation of a medium-term fiscal framework was intended to help maintain debt levels on a downward trend, with the goal of reaching 40 percent of GDP in about 10 years. To support this framework, in early 2004 the debt management office decided to revise its strategic target defined at the beginning of the decade; it increased the target share of domestic debt in the total debt portfolio from 40 percent to 50 percent to reduce exposure to currency movements, and to lower refinancing risk by extending the average maturity of the domestic debt portfolio.

Progress in debt management reform was slowest in those countries whose governments were unable to control the debt dynamics and where actions toward fiscal improvements weakened. For example, in Nicaragua, political tensions rose sharply from early 2004, contributing to an environment that pushed fiscal consolidation offtrack. Nicaragua's decision not to move the fiscal responsibility legislation forward was based on the authorities' assessment that it would not achieve the desired result, given the prevailing political environment. In Sri Lanka, a change in government in 2004 slowed the momentum for reforms initiated by the previous government. In Lebanon, continued internal tensions and fractious politics prevented much of the Paris II policy agenda from being implemented; as a result, debt levels did not decline.

Those pilot countries that managed to stabilize or reduce their debt levels did so through sustained fiscal consolidation and strong economic growth. To support these outcomes and reduce vulnerability to shocks, actions to strengthen public debt management have been a priority in Bulgaria, Indonesia, and Tunisia.[12] These countries illustrate that positive debt dynamics can be generated by well-coordinated implementation of sound fiscal, monetary, and debt management policies.

Bulgaria and Tunisia's initiatives for strengthening debt management followed track records of prudent macroeconomic management, which helped improve the governments' access to international capital markets. In Tunisia, the introduction of an action plan for public debt management was part of the government's strategy to maintain a stable macroeconomic framework—including the achievement of a debt-to-GDP ratio of 45 percent by 2009. In Bulgaria, authorities developed the first debt management strategy for the period 2003–05, coinciding with the time frame for the three-year budget framework and macroeconomic forecasts, while setting a longer-term goal of acceding to the European Union in 2007. In Indonesia, to maintain the downward trajectory of the public debt toward 30 percent of GDP by 2009, the debt management strategy rested on measures to help ensure that poor debt management did not jeopardize this objective.

In those pilot countries where domestic debt management functions are carried out at the central bank (because of insufficient capacity at the finance ministry), the separation of debt management and monetary policy remains a challenge, because the central bank is expected to continue debt management responsibilities for the foreseeable future (Kenya, Pakistan, Sri Lanka, and Zambia). These countries adopted a two-pronged approach to first, strengthen the agency agreement and coordination arrangements between the central bank and finance ministry, and second, ensure that capacity is built in the finance ministry over the medium term. For example, Lebanon and Zambia each established a high-level committee between the central bank and the finance ministry to ensure that both institutions understand each other's concerns and policy priorities. In Sri Lanka, progress in reforming monetary policy implementation and development of the domestic debt market has helped reduce the policy tensions.[13] In Lebanon, the central bank's influence on yields across the entire yield curve was reduced with the establishment in November 2003 of a new arrangement in which the bank compiles bids for the finance ministry to make decisions on auction allocation. In Pakistan, it was recommended that monetary policy operate at the short end of the yield curve, while leaving the rest of the curve up to the market.

In pilot countries where both the central bank and the finance ministry issued debt, short-term actions to diminish market uncertainty about policy signaling were taken.[14] For example, Costa Rica closely coordinated the issuance program by introducing joint auctions for short-term government and central bank debt, a regular calendar, well-defined instruments, and a clear process. Nonetheless, unpredictability in the issuance program for the medium-term segment of the market persisted, owing to the lack of a joint debt issuance strategy, which in turn was the result of a lack of consensus on whether the central bank should issue longer-dated securities at all. Because a full recapitalization of the central bank was not politically feasible at the time, a proposal to transfer the annual quasi-fiscal deficit to the government's budget, by way of annual transfers of government securities to the central bank, was being considered. Over the medium term, a resolution of the recapitalization of the central bank will help reduce the potential for conflicts between monetary policy and debt management and thereby enhance the independence of the central bank and its policy credibility. In Indonesia, the central bank is planning a fundamental reform of its monetary policy framework toward the adoption of inflation targeting, and includes the replacement of central bank securities with government securities in conducting open market operations.

Reforms in cash management to ease the constraints on the timing of bond sales caused by the timing of receipts and payments are being considered in Bulgaria, Colombia, Croatia, Indonesia, and Tunisia.

As a first step, Bulgaria and Croatia have moved cash management functions out of the budget department to the debt management unit, while Colombia has merged the unit that managed cash in the treasury with the debt management unit in the finance ministry. Such consolidation not only yields greater operational efficiency, it also allows market intelligence to be gathered on a daily basis. In Indonesia and Tunisia, consideration was being given to using short-dated cash management bills to smooth the volume of bond issuance.

Indonesia's and Lebanon's ministries of finance are upgrading their cash flow forecasting capability for expenditures and revenues. They also plan to establish a single treasury account and to streamline their payments and receipts processes to reduce the incidence of idle balances and the level of debt and debt servicing. Tunisia's government is also working to improve forecasting capacity by extending the capabilities of its financial management system and enhancing information provision from the tax collection office. Improvements in government cash flow forecasting will also help smooth the profile of government auction volumes.

CONCLUSIONS AND INSIGHTS

Fiscal and budget planning in the pilot-program countries was frequently undertaken with a one-year time horizon, which reinforced a short-term approach to public debt management. The absence of an explicit debt management strategy that takes into account the management of risk increased the likelihood that the borrowing program would be structured to meet short-term budget needs. A number of pilot countries have high public debt levels and interest expenses of up to 50 percent of government revenues. In these circumstances, debt managers may encounter pressure to produce cost savings, irrespective of the impact on long-run risk.[15]

Although fiscal sustainability analysis is the responsibility of fiscal policy advisors, debt managers are able to provide a richer understanding of how changes in financial variables can affect government finances. However, debt managers' input into fiscal sustainability analysis in the pilot countries has been minimal.

Improving the quality of public debt management can achieve only so much; ultimately, fiscal policy determines the borrowing requirement and is therefore the main influence on the stock of debt over time. To maximize the benefit of measures to improve public debt management, such as a medium-term strategy and greater transparency, a government should have in place a similar framework for fiscal policy. Some countries have unrealistic expectations that improving their debt management will solve their debt problems, when, of course, these can only be addressed by fiscal policy measures.

Coordination at the operational level helps ensure that forecasts of debt servicing cost are prepared on a basis consistent with the rest of the budget, both for assumptions and for budget balance projections. Most of the 12 pilot countries have reasonable coordination, although the quality of the forecasting varies.

Coordination between debt management and monetary policy is particularly important in countries with less developed domestic government debt markets. In several pilot countries, the main instrument of monetary policy was issuing debt in the primary market, that is, using the same instrument as the public debt manager. The scale of these operations was large in some countries, because governments had not fully financed their deficits in the past, forcing central banks to issue considerable debt to mop up excess liquidity. In these circumstances, coordination with debt managers may occur in a strained environment. The central bank wishes to shift its excess liabilities to the government, while the government is reluctant to bear the fiscal consequences of doing so.[16]

Conflict between debt management and monetary policy, or the potential for such conflict, was seen as likely to occur when the central bank takes a leading role in managing domestic debt. In these circumstances, the central bank may face pressure to reduce government debt servicing costs by providing direct financing, or to maintain interest rates at lower levels than desirable for price stability. The central bank's role often derived from necessity, because of limited capacity in finance ministries, and efforts to improve capacity can only occur slowly over time. Shorter term measures include agency agreements between central banks and ministries of finance that clarify decision-making rules for domestic debt management and greater transparency around the implementation of monetary policy.

Poor coordination with cash management hinders effective domestic debt management. In a number of pilot-program countries, the timing of domestic borrowing was determined by the government's cash flow needs, because there was no active cash management or instruments to smooth the short-run peaks and troughs in the government's cash flows. Thus, the size and composition of government bond auctions varied greatly from month to month. This unpredictability, in turn, undermined efforts to develop the domestic debt market. To improve management of domestic borrowing, reform efforts may need to extend into the areas of budget execution and cash management.

Lack of progress in coordinating debt management with fiscal and monetary management, as well as cash management in several pilot countries, has highlighted that reforming debt management in isolation can achieve only so much and that more comprehensive reforms can be mutually reinforcing.

Governance

he governance structure supporting public debt management should delineate clear roles and responsibilities for the institutions involved, be guided by checks and balances, and include clear reporting lines. The main institutions are the debt management office (DMO), normally located in the finance ministry as a separate department; the minister of finance; parliament; auditors; and often the central bank.

The DMO's role is to raise the required amount of funding, record and service the debt, and manage the costs and risks of the debt portfolio. In its daily operations and analytical work, the DMO should be somewhat independent, from both the finance minister and parliament. Otherwise there is a risk, particularly during periods of budget constraints, that short-term cost minimization will override longer-term risk considerations.

The debt management strategy embodies the government's preferred risk tolerance, which can vary over time depending on such factors as the strength of the economy, budget forecasts, and the stage of development of the domestic government debt market. Because this is a political issue, closely linked to fiscal policy, the debt management strategy is generally decided by the finance minister, with input from the DMO. The strategy puts into operation the objectives for debt management set by the parliament and provides a framework for delegation of authority from the finance minister to the DMO. Under this framework, the DMO is required to report back yearly to the minister of finance on how successful it has been in achieving the determined strategy. In turn, the minister should report back to parliament.

Stemming from its legislative and financial powers, the parliament has the ultimate legal authority to borrow on behalf of the state. The parliament also typically sets borrowing limits, normally in the form of an annual limit in connection with the approval of the fiscal budget.[1] The role of parliament in public debt management differs among countries. Sound practice, however, calls for the parliament to delegate its borrowing power while at the same time determining the long-term objectives of debt management and requiring at least yearly reports from the government on how these goals have been achieved. The most common objectives are ensuring that the central government's financing needs are met, minimizing borrowing costs, keeping risk at an acceptable level, and supporting the development of domestic debt markets (see OECD 2002). Based on these objectives, the minister of finance then determines the strategy by considering trade-offs between the expected cost and risk, as well as the constraints faced by the government.

The supreme audit institution is the taxpayers' independent and professional watchdog. The audit of government debt management should include evaluation of the control environment (including the organizational structure and information technology systems), an operational risk assessment, evaluation of control activities, evaluation of the information and communication flows, and evaluation of the monitoring of the internal controls undertaken by the internal auditors (see International Organization of Supreme Audit Institutions 2000).

The role of the central bank in government debt management differs across countries. In a system with a DMO, the role of the central bank is limited to acting as its agent. Common functions of the central bank as agent are to run the domestic government bill and bond auctions and serve as paying agent and depository for the central government.

A stylized view of the line of authority and delegation of responsibilities, as well as reporting back to the authorities, is depicted in figure 5.1.

DEBT MANAGEMENT OBJECTIVES AND THE LEGAL FRAMEWORK

Leading debt managers generally agree on the benefits of having explicit debt management objectives. Objectives not only clarify the aims of debt management activities, but are also a prerequisite for formulating a debt management strategy and for evaluating its implementation.

Good governance requires that legislation should, at a minimum, clarify the authority to borrow and issue new debt, invest, and undertake

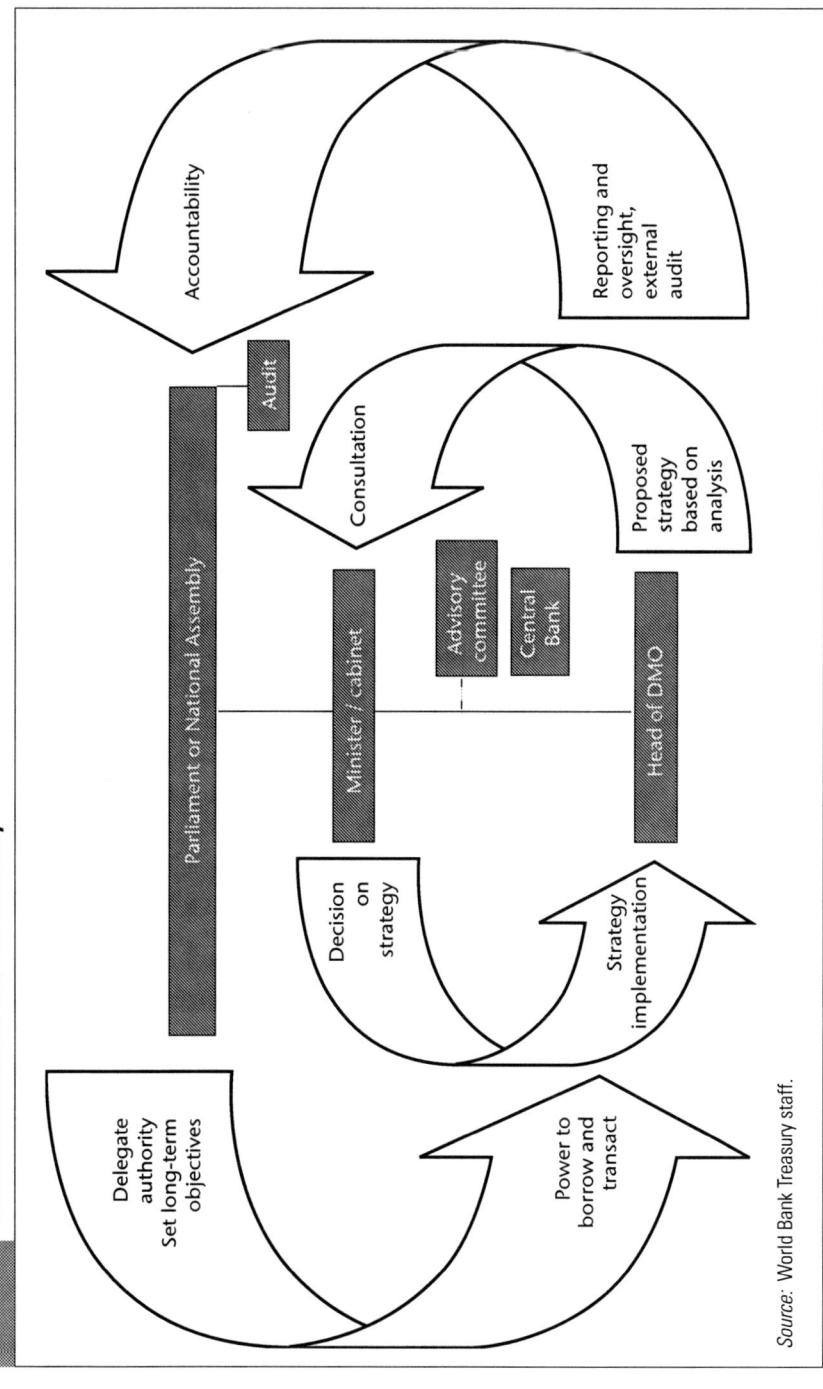

FIGURE 5.1 Governance Structure and Accountability

Source: World Bank Treasury staff.

transactions on the government's behalf (including refinancing existing debt). Authority is normally stipulated either through borrowing authority legislation with a preset limit, or through a debt ceiling.

Diagnostics in Pilot Countries

Few pilot countries had a clearly stated objective for public debt management to guide the debt management strategy. Only Bulgaria (in the debt management strategy document) and Nicaragua (in the Public Debt Law) had clearly stated objectives to fund the government's needs while minimizing costs in a way consistent with a prudent level of risk. Costa Rica and Lebanon state their objectives as reducing both the volume of debt and the cost of servicing it, but in the absence of an explicit consideration of the risk of the debt portfolio, this objective relates more to fiscal policy in the short run.

Most pilot-program countries met the minimum requirement for legislation in public debt management—that is, clarifying who has the authority to borrow. In most cases, the authority rested with the finance minister. The minister generally has the power to authorize transactions, but frequently in the context of an annual program set by the cabinet. In Bulgaria and Croatia, decision making was collective and the full government made the final debt management decisions.

In Sri Lanka, an accumulation of legislation over the years led to dispersed responsibility for borrowing. Although ultimate authority generally lies with the minister of finance or the president, the central bank was consulted or acted as agent. By convention, the cabinet might also be involved in decision making. In Lebanon, the authority to borrow was split between the ministry of finance and a separate executive agency (the Council for Reconstruction and Development). In Costa Rica, the finance minister and central bank governor were empowered to issue debt, but the central bank issued in its own name rather than that of the republic. Zambia's law, however, does not specify who has the authority to contract debt on behalf of the republic.

Whether the ultimate responsibility rests with the finance minister or the cabinet, specific authority is still needed to enter into transactions at the operational level. In most countries, such authority was specified in secondary legislation. For example, Croatian legislation specified the cabinet's delegation of responsibility for implementing the cabinet's borrowing decisions to the "debt manager".[2] Bulgaria does not have any decision-making delegation from the deputy minister to the debt directorate.

The laws in all but Lebanon and Tunisia specified overall debt ceilings either as a percentage of GDP or in nominal amounts (Zambia).[3] In Kenya, debt ceilings were specified for external debt but there were no limits on domestic debt.

The pilot countries also set annual borrowing limits, in most cases in the annual budget law (Bulgaria, Colombia, Costa Rica, Croatia, Indonesia, Lebanon, Sri Lanka, and Tunisia). In Pakistan, the annual limit was set in the Fiscal Responsibility and Debt Limitation Act, in the form of a debt reduction path. Annual limits on guarantees were specified in the laws of Bulgaria, Colombia, Croatia, Pakistan, and Tunisia.

In most cases, annual borrowing limits were set in net terms. In Indonesia, however, even though a recent law for borrowing through securities specified limits in net terms, the parliament initially continued to express it in gross terms.[4] This created an aversion to issuing short-term debt, which limits flexibility and the development of efficient cash management.

In addition, in Indonesia and Lebanon, annual borrowing limits for different types of loans and instruments—for example, domestic bank financing, issuance of securities, and borrowing through loans—were also defined in the annual budget law. These amounts can be exceeded only through amendments in the budget law, before the borrowing occurs.[5] Setting individual limits for different types of borrowing constrains the debt manager's ability to execute an agreed-on debt management strategy based on the most cost-effective instruments at particular times.

Restrictions on the issuance of guarantees were in place in Bulgaria, Colombia, Croatia, Kenya, Pakistan, Sri Lanka, Tunisia, and Zambia. In Kenya, Sri Lanka, and Zambia, no loan guarantees can be issued without the approval of the parliament and all must be signed by the finance minister. Although Costa Rica limited budgetary issuance of direct debt, it set no limits on the budgetary issuance of guarantees.[6]

The budget laws in Bulgaria, Nicaragua, and Tunisia specify a multiyear framework for formulation of the budget; Colombia, Croatia, Pakistan, and Sri Lanka have also recently begun multiyear budgeting. The budget laws in the other pilot countries, however, were focused on financing the government from year to year and ensuring that the borrowing was duly authorized, which does not support managing debt in a medium-term framework.

One of the main features of the pilot countries (except for Bulgaria, Croatia, and Nicaragua) was the multiplicity of laws relating to various aspects of public debt. Although far from comprehensive, appendix table A.1 illustrates the degree of fragmentation of the legal framework. Such fragmentation is not necessarily a major problem, so long as the laws are consistent with each other. However, multiple layers of legislation, coupled with poor drafting and insufficient linkage with earlier laws, can

- lock in multiple responsibilities for debt management and perpetuate a lack of coordination;
- increase the scope for different interpretations, creating uncertainty about the responsibilities and accountabilities for managing the overall debt portfolio; and
- create differences in the level of oversight for different types of borrowing.

In most cases, the collection of laws reflects the historical evolution of sources of borrowing and amendments for specific operational reasons.

In several pilot countries, the parliament, president, or prime minister exerted greater control over external debt than over domestic debt. In Kenya, the national assembly approved the maximum external indebtedness while it imposed no limits on the amount of domestic debt (which is at the discretion of the finance minister).

Bulgaria, Colombia, Lebanon, Nicaragua, and Tunisia exercised greater control over external debt by requiring parliamentary or presidential approval for each transaction. For the government of Tunisia to borrow in the international capital markets, the exact financing terms had to be decided six to eight weeks before the launch of the transaction, which is clearly not possible. To manage this situation, the central bank borrows in foreign markets in its own name. Following each transaction, the approval of parliament is sought to enter into an identical borrowing from the central bank (table 5.1).

Two reasons have been cited for why parliaments might exercise such controls:

- Because currency crises have been caused in part by excessive contracting of external debt, parliaments feel the need to control the amount of foreign-currency debt issued by the government.
- Because foreign borrowing contracts normally include a jurisdiction clause, where the borrower submits to the jurisdiction of foreign courts or international arbitration, parliamentary approval is needed.

Such considerations, however, do not mean that transaction-by-transaction approval by the executive or legislative branch is a good solution, because it limits the flexibility to efficiently execute an agreed-on borrowing program.

TABLE 5.1   Authorizations Required by Parliament and Other Institutions for External Borrowing

Country	Requirements
Bulgaria	The National Assembly approves and ratifies individual borrowing transactions in foreign markets.
Colombia	In addition to the approval required by the legislative committee, the central bank is also involved in authorizing individual funding transactions.[a] The authorization process for individual capital market transactions involves a number of government entities and committees. These include not only the Debt Directorate, but also the central bank, the National Planning Department, and the National Council of Economic and Social Policy, in addition to the Inter-parliamentary Commission.
Costa Rica	The general debt law requires explicit congressional approval for each external debt issuance. However, in December 1999, the Legislative Assembly approved Law 7970, a five-year public debt law authorizing US$1.45 billion in foreign debt issuance over five years.
Croatia	The cabinet approves the proposals for new borrowing and refinancing of domestic and external debt coming from the finance ministry at its weekly meeting.
Kenya	Parliamentary control is carried out after the fact, and the finance minister is required to inform the National Assembly of every loan transaction as soon as practicable after the loan is arranged.
Lebanon	The Council of Ministers approves the issuance of Eurobonds by resolution (either loan by loan or a series of loans) up to the ceiling set in the budget law for that year. These approvals specify the volume of bonds to be issued, but not the tenor or rate, which are decided by the finance minister. Each foreign-currency loan relating to reconstruction and development projects from multilateral and bilateral donors contracted by the Council for Reconstruction and Development must be ratified by parliament.
Nicaragua	The constitution requires the National Assembly to explicitly approve each external debt operation.
Sri Lanka	The cabinet's economic policy committee must give approval before any ministry or agency enters into discussions or negotiations with any foreign donor agencies.[b]
Tunisia	The constitution establishes that decisions related to government borrowing and financial commitments shall be adopted as a law. The Judicial Council interprets this article as requiring prior approval of the assembly for every external debt contract of the government, including the precise financial terms and conditions. Hence, the authorization process for external borrowing (where every transaction must have prior approval of the assembly) is significantly different from that for domestic borrowing. For domestic borrowing, the borrowing instrument is designed by presidential decree and individual transactions are undertaken by the finance ministry at its own discretion, within the envelope of the annual finance law.

Source: World Bank Treasury staff.

a. In Colombia, public sector external and domestic bond issues require prior approval from the central bank board. The Central Bank Law of 1992 gives the bank the authority to regulate capital markets and public debt issues. It does so by establishing that the bank is responsible for determining the financial conditions under which public entities shall issue or buy securities, with the aim of ensuring that these operations take place at market prices. If those conditions are not met, the corresponding securities cannot be issued or placed. In practice, central bank intervention in public debt policy has only not approved the issuance of T-bills, although more recently it did authorize the finance ministry (treasury) to begin issuing a small annual volume of T-bills.

b. The Economic Policy Committee has since ceased meeting and the External Resource Department of the ministry of finance has the sole responsibility for negotiating and discussing with foreign donor agencies.

Action Plans and Reform Experiences

Pilot countries have taken specific actions to implement reform in the legal framework. These include

- consolidation of laws,
- use of secondary legislation,
- modernization of existing debt laws, and
- resolution of the asymmetric legislative control of domestic and external debt.

As with reform efforts to develop a debt management strategy, specification and implementation of legal reforms in pilot countries was characterized by institutional difficulties and different rates of progression. Nevertheless, pilot countries took pragmatic actions, particularly by using secondary laws, to facilitate work on the other components of debt management reform. In pilot countries where new public debt laws were drafted, greatest attention was given to an accountability framework within which to delegate authority for debt management.

Three pilot countries introduced consolidated laws. Croatia passed a consolidated Budget Act (2003) that includes a separate chapter on debt management and guarantees. In Nicaragua, the Public Debt Law was approved by Congress in 2003 following Heavily Indebted Poor Countries debt forgiveness; Bulgaria also adopted a modern debt law in 2002 before the pilot program. This law, separate from the budget laws, supports debt management in a medium-term framework by requiring that a three-year strategy paper be prepared and presented to parliament and that the minister report on the results of the previous year.

The authorities in Colombia (box 5.1), Lebanon, and Sri Lanka have drafted debt management laws, but these have not been passed by parliament.

The authorities in Indonesia, Lebanon, Tunisia, and Zambia reported that comprehensive legal reform was not an option, at least in the short run. One of the obstacles to comprehensive reform cited by the Indonesian authorities was the multiplicity of departments that could be involved in the bilateral and multilateral external borrowing process. This hampered consensus building on content and weakened the momentum for consolidated debt legislation.

Because of the practical difficulties of enacting wholesale legal change, some finance ministers have found it more convenient to use secondary legislation—including decrees, regulations, administrative laws,

BOX 5.1 **Rationale for a Consolidated Law on Public Debt Management: Colombia**

The legal group of the debt management unit in Colombia proposed creating a consolidated general law on public debt management to

- establish a guiding principle and one coherent framework for public sector indebtedness, as opposed to the existing multiple and dispersed bylaws and decrees;
- fend off political pressures in executing public debt policy;
- achieve a conceptual framework for debt management that allows the *Dirección General de Crédito Público* to adequately control subnational government debt;
- provide an adequate legal framework for new and complex forms of financing and active debt management operations; and
- establish clear responsibilities for the various government units participating in debt management, so that ultimately the choice of funding source and financial conditions are determined by the central government.

However, because of the lack of political support for the draft law in the finance ministry, the law was not presented to Congress. The legal group may again propose a new draft public debt law.

Source: World Bank Treasury staff.

and internal regulations—which is more flexible and can be enacted more quickly. For example, in Croatia, debt management objectives were included in the regulation on the internal structure of the finance ministry. In Indonesia, the authorities issued a ministerial decree to establish a coordination team to work on reforming debt management and domestic government debt market development. This, however, runs the risk of temporarily adding to an already complicated and fragmented legal framework.

In several pilot countries, however, debt laws have been modernized to meet new borrowing requirements and accommodate new government debt instruments. For example, the 1925 Indonesian Treasury Law, amended in 1968, was replaced by an updated legal framework with the passage of the State Finances Law (2003), the Government Securities Law (2002), and the State Treasury Law (2004). The Government Securities Law was required because the government rapidly expanded domestic borrowing following the financial crisis in the late 1990s, and because external borrowing was diversified away from bilateral and multilateral sources toward funding in the international markets.

Adequate control over the volume of foreign-currency debt can be implemented either through permanent debt ceilings or annual borrowing limits in budget legislation. Concerns about the types of foreign borrowing (for example, whether market borrowing is permissible) can be addressed through a debt management strategy that is agreed on at the cabinet or parliamentary level. This framework gives individual ministers or debt managers the flexibility to implement market transactions within short time frames. Clearly, such an approach is practical only where accountability and oversight arrangements are sufficiently strong to allow ministers or ministry officials to approve individual transactions within agreed-on parameters.

Costa Rica's experience also illustrates how a country can revise its practices. The general debt law required explicit congressional approval for each external debt issue, but the authorities issued a law that temporarily superseded the general debt law. It authorizes the finance ministry to issue external debt of up to US$1.45 billion over five years without requiring congressional approval for individual transactions.

ORGANIZATIONAL ARRANGEMENTS

Sound public debt management requires an institutional structure that clearly delineates roles, responsibilities, and reporting channels for the relevant institutions. Consolidating debt management functions into one department or directorate avoids duplication of functions, strengthens accountability, and reduces coordination and informational requirements. It also facilitates the analysis and development of a strategy for the aggregate debt portfolio, because one entity is clearly mandated to perform this role and maintains the information to undertake it.

Within this framework, some operations can be contracted out but not without spelling out the responsibilities and performance standards in an agency agreement.

When consolidating debt management responsibilities into one entity, clear internal divisions of responsibilities are needed to reduce operational risk.[7] In particular, separation between front- and back-office activities is critical for reducing the risk of fraud in any organization undertaking financial market transactions. In turn, in more advanced operations, the separation of front- and middle-office activities ensures the independence of those setting and monitoring the risk management framework from those responsible for executing market transactions.

Debt management units require well-articulated responsibilities for staff, clear monitoring and control policies, and clear documentation of procedures. In addition, because many debt management functions involve market contact and access to market information, a code of conduct and conflict-of-interest guidelines are necessary.

Finally, sound business recovery procedures should be in place to mitigate the risk that debt management activities might be severely disrupted by natural disasters, social unrest, or acts of terrorism.

Diagnostics in Pilot Countries

One of the main features common to pilot countries was that debt management responsibilities and functions were scattered across institutions and departments (appendix table A.2). The problems that arose because of this dispersed organization have been described in earlier chapters, particularly the impact on the development of a debt management strategy (chapter 3) and its possible contributions to policy conflicts (chapter 4).

The location of issuance or borrowing functions (front-office responsibilities) across institutions and within institutions varied across pilot countries, but one of the common patterns observed was by funding source: by domestic and external debt (Kenya, Lebanon, Pakistan, and Zambia); or by market or official source (Croatia, Indonesia, Sri Lanka, and Tunisia). Both the ministry of finance and the central bank were responsible for managing part of the debt in Costa Rica, Kenya, Nicaragua, Pakistan, Sri Lanka, Tunisia, and Zambia. Other institutions, including a ministry responsible for economic development, were also involved in Lebanon, Sri Lanka, and Tunisia. Back-office functions were similarly scattered, often reflecting the front-office organizational structures (appendix table A.2).

In some pilot countries, responsibilities were divided by the tenor of borrowing. In Colombia, for example, the Directorate of Public Credit was responsible for issuing longer-dated debt while the treasury was responsible for shorter-dated debt. Despite problems with multiple issuers, this division might be better than two or more government issuers competing in the same market segment, particularly if they are to serve as policy instruments. Multiple government issuers contribute to market fragmentation, which undermines efforts to develop the domestic debt market through liquid securities that can serve as reference points in the yield curve.

The reasons for the distribution of functions across different organizations were largely historical, in the same way that new legislation was introduced as new types of borrowing became available and new departments or entities were created to manage them. In some cases (see chapter 4), the allocation of responsibilities was reinforced by capacity constraints in finance ministries, leaving the central bank to perform many functions more as principal, rather than as agent.

Most of the pilot countries clearly distinguished between the transactions execution responsibilities of the front office and the deal confirmations (or deal verifications) and settlements responsibilities of the back office. In several pilot countries (Croatia, Kenya, and Pakistan), however, debt transactions were entered into and verified by the same unit and the separation of responsibilities was not achieved.

Although the DMO was notionally organized along functional lines in several countries, in practice, the functions actually performed did not conform to generally understood norms. For example, in Costa Rica, the front office in the treasury was responsible for a number of noncore activities, including validation of the data entry of external debt, authorization of debt of public entities, and tax devolutions for tax-exempt investors. The front office in Croatia performed tasks normally considered back-office functions, including maintaining details of the guarantees portfolio and the T-bill register. The primary responsibility of the back office was to enter details of payment requests into the Systems Applications and Products in Data Processing (SAP) system for forwarding to the Budget Execution Section for approval. Data given by the creditors in the payment reminders were being checked against the data in the debt management system, and the payments data were entered into the SAP system.

Action Plans and Reform Experiences

The reforms implemented in the pilot countries included

- consolidation of debt management functions into one DMO, either within the finance ministry or from the central bank to the finance ministry;
- setting up new units to perform responsibilities not carried out by existing units; and
- improving coordination between different units responsible for debt management.

Croatia and Colombia have addressed the fragmentation of their organizational arrangements by consolidating these functions. The Croatian government designed a new organizational structure for its Debt Management Sector (DMS) using the standard front-middle-back office configuration. Also, Croatia's reform program lays out plans to document work processes within the DMS, as well as organizational guidelines determining the internal division of responsibilities and decision making. The first step, taken in January 2005, was transferring the cash management functions from the Budget Execution Section to the DMS. A medium-term goal is to move the borrowing activities of the International Financial Institutions Department to the DMS.

Colombia gave priority to addressing the overlapping debt issuance functions in the Directorate General of Public Credit and the treasury. The objective was to support the development of both a more liquid domestic debt market and a coherent debt management strategy. However, rather than consolidate debt management responsibilities in one unit, the Colombian authorities' initial response was to coordinate the design of a joint debt management strategy. The treasury and the Directorate General of Public Credit were nonetheless merged in the fall of 2003 for greater administrative efficiency.

In 2003, Indonesia began to create a new Directorate General of Treasury, which included bringing the two debt management departments in the finance ministry under one umbrella. The organizational structure within the treasury continued to be based on source of financing rather than on functions: one department was responsible for managing domestic- and foreign-market securities borrowing, and the other for managing external loans from official sources. In 2006, a new finance minister took a step further by consolidating the two departments responsible for debt management under a Directorate General for Public Debt Management.

In pilot-program countries where the central bank was responsible for managing domestic debt, attempts to transfer debt management responsibilities from the central bank to the finance ministry were made. The results, however, were more setbacks than progress, given the opposition within the central banks to devolve responsibilities and the frequent lack of capacity to manage the new responsibilities in the ministries.

The impetus for public debt management reform in Sri Lanka came in 2000–01, when the central bank embarked on a fundamental restructuring. The goal of the restructuring was for the bank to transform itself into a "modern central bank" focused on price stability and financial system stability. Among a number of measures, the central bank decided to devolve noncore functions, including domestic public debt management. A focus group was convened to examine the future of public debt management; the focus group uncovered a conflict between the objectives of monetary policy and public debt management, given the decision-making structures within the central bank (Sri Lanka 2001). The diagnostic report completed during the pilot program supported the initiative to consolidate public debt management in a single department or office. The move to devolve domestic debt management from the central bank, however, lost momentum because of capacity limitations and competing priorities for resources in the finance ministry, and, ultimately, a change in government. However, the External Resources Department responsible for the management of external debt (from bilateral and multilateral sources) has been transferred from the Ministry of Policy Development and Implementation to the finance ministry.

The central bank of Zambia agreed to transfer responsibility for domestic borrowing to the Investment and Debt Management Department (IDM) in the ministry of finance. However, because building the necessary capacity at the ministry of finance was expected to take some time, the central bank had to continue managing domestic debt in the meantime. The reform plan envisioned the signing of an agency agreement defining the functions of the ministry of finance and the central bank, clarifying the responsibilities of each institution. The reform plan also specified a transition plan to gradually increase the involvement of IDM in the decision-making process, initially by having IDM participate when deciding cutoff prices at the auctions.

The central banks of Costa Rica and Nicaragua have been eager to transfer debt management responsibilities to the ministries of finance and stop issuing debt in their own names, because the accumulation of large quasi-fiscal deficits has begun to affect the credibility of monetary policy. In both countries, the finance ministries and central banks agreed that debt management functions should be consolidated in the ministries over the medium term. However, reforms to recapitalize the central banks and enable them to stop issuing their own securities could only be achieved over the medium term. The authorities thus decided that, in the short run, debt issuance would continue to be a joint responsibility, while they placed priority on building capacity in the finance ministry.

While the Tunisian authorities have set a medium-term goal of consolidating debt management activities in the treasury, the constitutional constraint that limits the ability of the ministry of finance to issue in the external capital market has meant that in the short run, external debt issuance responsibilities remain in the central bank. The central bank has also accumulated considerable expertise in this area.

To act on the priority of developing a debt management strategy, which would require building or acquiring additional technical expertise, several pilot countries have sought interim solutions. These have included setting up entirely new units, rather than restructuring the functions performed by existing departments. Pakistan established the Debt Policy Coordination Office, the initial responsibility of which was debt analysis and risk management, development of a unified database for public debt, and foreign-currency commercial borrowing. Sri Lanka considered a similar approach in the face of growing resistance to changing the functions of existing organizations.

While a first-best solution might have been to implement institutional reforms to consolidate debt management functions, in some of the countries the authorities concluded this would require a longer time frame. As a result, the reform plans specified improved coordination as a first step. For example, in Costa Rica coordination between the finance ministry and the central bank was formalized by the heads of the two institutions, who signed a memorandum of understanding, and agreed to a work program to develop a joint debt management strategy. The memorandum of understanding established an executive committee and a technical committee, whose functions were defined in the document. This interim solution envisaged that both the finance ministry and the central bank would continue to be issuers of debt. Over the medium term, the reform plan specified that as the central bank's quasi-fiscal deficit was addressed by the government, and the central bank phased itself out of issuing debt and toward implementing open market operations, debt management responsibilities would reside solely in the finance ministry.

The Indonesian authorities initially considered institutional reform to be difficult to implement and issued a ministerial decree establishing a coordination team to work on reforming debt management and debt market development. The working group consisted of staff from the two departments responsible for debt management in the ministry of finance and the central bank.

In Nicaragua, a debt committee was created to institutionalize public debt management decision making. It will also increase coordination between the central bank and the ministry of finance on debt issuance and management policies and activities.

Coordination was a challenge in other pilot countries. One of the obstacles was departmental and institutional rivalry and a lack of commitment by ministers. In three pilot countries, the head of the debt office resisted proposals to formalize the strategy and to create an executive debt management committee that would discuss it. Also, over longer time frames, coordination mechanisms can become less effective because they often rely on the goodwill of the officials involved at the time. With departures of key personalities, coordination committees can suddenly stop meeting; such was the experience with Colombia's debt committee in the 1990s.

Another obstacle has been the weak institutional capacity in the ministries of finance. In Zambia, an interinstitutional coordination team, consisting of officials from the ministry of finance and planning and the central bank, was created to conduct a joint analysis and design a debt management strategy. However, because of the ministry's weak capacity, the staffs of neither institution have attended the coordination meetings.

ACCOUNTABILITY, TRANSPARENCY, AND AUDITING

Accountability and transparency to the public through disclosure of activities and outcomes are integral to the exercise of powers vested through the delegation of authority. As with monetary and fiscal policies (see IMF 2000, 2001), accountability and transparency in implementing public debt management provide two main benefits:

- If the goals and instruments of policy are known to the public (financial markets) and if the authorities make a credible commitment to meeting them, the effectiveness of debt management is reinforced.
- Transparency can enhance good governance through greater accountability of the institutions involved in public debt management. To this end, the public needs to receive regular information on the stock and composition of the public debt, as well as on the government's overall financial position. Important aspects of debt management operations, such as objectives, financing requirements, and strategy, should be publicly disclosed.

Diagnostics in Pilot Countries

A government's overall financial reporting does not always include the stock and composition of public debt. For example, in Indonesia and Lebanon, the government's financial statements, which are officially audited and presented to parliament, relate to budget revenue and expenditure flows only, and do not include information on debt stock and its financial characteristics. To rectify this, Indonesia's new law on public financial management specifies that the financial statements must include a balance sheet by 2006.

Specific reporting on public debt by the finance minister to the parliament was required by law in many pilot countries (table 5.2). The laws required the production and presentation to parliament of the annual debt policy statement (Nicaragua and Pakistan), annual debt report (Indonesia and Nicaragua), reporting on the status of government debt

(Bulgaria and Croatia), and policy guidelines for the indebtedness of the rest of the public sector (Nicaragua). However, Nicaragua had not produced such documents.

In most pilot-program countries an auditor general was responsible for auditing government accounts and reporting directly to parliament. In Bulgaria, Kenya, and Sri Lanka, the constitution explicitly protects the independence of external auditors. In Bulgaria, the National Audit Office Act specifies that, among other things, the office shall audit "the formation and management of the state debt and the use of debt instruments." In Croatia, the State Audit Office audits all activities of the finance ministry and everything covered in the state budget. The Supreme Auditor in

TABLE 5.2   Reporting Requirements Specified in the Legal Framework

Country	Law	Specified reporting requirements
Bulgaria	Law on Government Debt	The finance minister is required to prepare an annual report on the state of the government debt. The annual report is then reviewed by the Council of Ministers and submitted to the National Assembly as an integral part of the government budget performance report for the respective year. The finance minister is also required to develop a three-year government debt management strategy, which should be approved by the Council of Ministers. In addition, the official information on the consolidated government and government guaranteed debt should be published on a monthly basis by the finance ministry in an official bulletin and on the Internet.
Croatia	Budget Act	The finance minister is required to prepare both annual and semiannual statements on the status of government debt, including information on any prepayments and the use of any financial derivatives. These reports must be delivered to the Croatian parliament as part of the government's report on budget execution.
Indonesia	Government Securities Law	The finance minister is required to prepare an "accountability report" on the management of government securities and to periodically publish information on the composition of securities and on debt management policies.
Kenya	Internal Loans Act, and the External Loans and Credits Act	The finance minister is required to report to the National Assembly on outstanding public indebtedness, broken down by the type of borrowing, at the end of each fiscal year. The minister is also required to report outstanding foreign borrowings at the end of the fiscal year, and to inform the assembly of every loan transaction as soon as practicable after the loan is arranged.

(continued)

TABLE 5.2 *continued*

Country	Law	Specified reporting requirements
Nicaragua	Public Debt Law	The minister of finance is required to submit an Annual Debt Policy statement to the president. The ministry of finance must also produce policy guidelines for the indebtedness of the rest of the public sector (other than the central government) and present them to the National Assembly as an integral part of the General Budget Law.[a]
Pakistan	Fiscal Responsibility and Debt Limitation Act	The government is required to present an annual debt policy statement to the National Assembly. The statement must include an assessment of the government's success or failure in meeting public debt targets. It must also include an evaluation of external and domestic borrowing strategies, an assessment of the nominal and real cost of external and domestic debt, an analysis of foreign currency exposure, an analysis of public debt trends, and information on guarantees and budgetary out-turns of guarantees and of all loans contracted.
Sri Lanka	Fiscal Management (Responsibility) Act	The following reports must be presented to parliament and to the general public by the finance minister within a given time frame: fiscal strategy statement, budget, economic and fiscal position report, and midyear fiscal position report.
Zambia	Loans and Guarantees Act	The government is required to include information in the financial report on the debt payments in the relevant year.

Source: World Bank Treasury staff.

a. While reporting and accountability facilitates delegation of authority, one of the main issues in Nicaragua was that the reporting structure foreseen in the law did not match the actual structure for delegation. While the National Assembly delegated to the finance ministry responsibility for debt management, the corresponding strategy designed by the finance ministry was presented for approval to the president. The finance minister was not obligated to report to the assembly on whether or how debt management was meeting the country's debt management objectives.

Indonesia conducts annual audits on the processing of debt transactions, including linkages with such other entities as the central bank, and also discusses the policy framework. In Lebanon, the Audit Court audits only annual budget execution reports. The Auditor General in Zambia produced annual reports on the accounts of the government but the most recent annual report was three years behind.

External auditors in some of the 12 pilot-program countries have called for improved debt management, citing the need to

▓ consolidate fragmented legislation and unify the definition of debt statistics (Bulgaria);

- establish a specialized unit to prepare and substantiate a mid-term strategy (Bulgaria);
- strengthen debt recording (Croatia);
- strengthen accounting and public debt reconciliation (Sri Lanka);
- improve coordination among entities responsible for debt management and consolidate debt management functions into one location that produces financial statements (Sri Lanka);
- address delays in releasing the accounts, sometimes by years (Sri Lanka); and
- remedy instances in which project disbursements or grants are made directly by donors to implementing agencies and the information is not transmitted to the treasury on a timely basis (Sri Lanka).

A case study in Zambia by the International Organization of Supreme Audit Institutions examined questions relating to the control environment, control activities, risk assessment, information and communication, and monitoring.[8] It found that improving these are a prerequisite for reliable debt reporting systems. In particular,

- continuous training and development in debt management is essential for debt managers,
- a strict code of conduct is meaningless if no action is taken when it is breached,
- prudent debt policies must be backed by operational manuals and guidelines that are kept up to date, and
- segregation of duties among authorization, recording, and custody of public debt resources is paramount, and must be combined with effective monitoring procedures.

The specialized nature of debt transactions and public debt management has been a challenge to auditors accustomed to analyzing the generic processes of government. Also, being the taxpayer's independent and professional watchdog did not always produce results. For example, the State Audit Office of Croatia complained about the standard of debt recording for 10 years but their reports were not acted on.

Some of the pilot countries reduced operational risk by documenting procedures. For example, in Indonesia and Sri Lanka, procedures manuals described every task performed in the debt office.[9] Having adequate processes and procedures is insufficient, however, if they are not followed at a higher level and if auditors' warnings and recommendations go unheeded. This is well illustrated by a corruption scandal in Kenya (box 5.2). Also, none of the countries had a code of conduct for

BOX 5.2 **The Anglo Leasing Corruption Scandal in Kenya**

The Anglo Leasing scandal involving the debt management department of the Kenyan finance ministry, which became public in the spring of 2004, was part of a pattern that had developed over several years. The scandal involved the use of many phantom entities to perpetrate fraud on the Kenyan taxpayer through nondelivery of goods and services and massive overpricing. A special audit report of the Controller and Auditor General (April 2006) showed that 18 security-related contracts similar to the Anglo Leasing contract had been signed by the government since 1997, with a total contract amount of US$751 million.

The contract signed with Anglo Leasing & Finance Limited was to finance, supply, and install a new "immigration security and documents control system." The commitment was made outside the government budgetary process and without any competitive bidding, and it was not possible to ascertain how the contract sum was determined. A comparison of the project implementation and credit repayment schedules indicated that the government was in effect funding the financiers and suppliers to finance the procurement of the goods and services due under the contracts, while also paying interest and other financing costs to the same financiers and suppliers.

Before the contract was signed by the then Permanent Secretary of Finance, the head of the Debt Management Department had approved the financial terms in a separate memo. Once the contract was signed, the financial terms were entered into the debt recording system by the Debt Management Department and the payments were effected by the same procedure used for servicing any other foreign debt.

The Attorney General's office checked the terms and conditions of the contract. It questioned some of the unfavorable clauses in the contract but the comments were apparently ignored.

The transaction constituted a breach of the agreement with the International Monetary Fund, which did not allow Kenya to contract any foreign debt on commercial terms as long as the Poverty Reduction and Growth Facility program was in place; in addition, its legality under the External Loans and Credits Act was questionable.

As a consequence of the scandal, the minister of finance, the two permanent secretaries who signed the contract, the financial secretary of the ministry of finance, and the head of the Debt Management Department, resigned.

In a report (March 2006) delivered to the Public Accounts Committee of the National Assembly, the new financial secretary stated: "Over the years, the institutional framework for contracting and managing external commercial loans collapsed. In the 1990s, contracting and managing commercial loans have not been done within the laid down framework. Spending ministries assumed the role of Treasury identifying and negotiating with possible financiers all aspects of the financing agreement. Treasury was used to only rubber-stamp agreements with limited knowledge of financiers. The failure to follow the laid down institutional arrangement in contracting commercial loans has led to major lapses in the overall management of public debt. Some of the resultant effects of this weakness in our debt management system are failure to fully comply with the law relating to external borrowing, loan contracts with very unfavourable terms, loss of expenditure control, and serious cases of fraud due to absence of due diligence" (report by permanent secretary/treasury to the public accounts committee on financing security projects through external borrowing, Monday, March 13, 2006, p. 2).

Source: World Bank Treasury staff.

staff, specific to debt management areas, providing guidance and controls on transacting in the market.

Action Plans and Reform Experiences

Specific actions taken by pilot countries to improve transparency and accountability include

- voluntary publication of information to increase transparency,
- publication of the debt management strategy,
- improvements to auditing capacity, and
- improvements to business processes and internal procedures.

While public financial reporting rules and laws can help institutionalize the accountability and transparency framework, the experiences of several pilot-program countries have demonstrated that the laws were not necessarily followed.

Some of the countries, however, have shown that changes to laws and regulations were not necessarily prerequisites for increasing transparency. In these cases, the authorities voluntarily produced information on the public debt to supplement data appearing in financial statements (Colombia, Indonesia, Lebanon, Tunisia, Sri Lanka, and Zambia). Several reasons underpin this improved transparency: increased internal needs for better information flows and the need to manage the risks of the debt portfolio (Bulgaria, Colombia, Lebanon, Tunisia, and Zambia); new bond issuance requiring credit ratings and information to be submitted to rating agencies, as well as increased demand coming from investors (Bulgaria, Colombia, Indonesia, and Lebanon);[10] and international and domestic creditors, as well as governments' subscription to the International Monetary Fund's Code of Good Practices on Fiscal Transparency, leading governments to increasingly publish more regular information (Bulgaria, Colombia, Croatia, Lebanon, Nicaragua, Pakistan, Sri Lanka, and Tunisia). Much of the information is now available on finance ministries' Web sites.

Turning to forward-looking information, Bulgaria is most advanced, having developed and published a comprehensive debt management strategy.[11] Colombia has had a strategy for its external debt portfolio for several years and the details are publicly available; in 2005, Colombia published its strategy for the total debt. Croatia, Indonesia, and Nicaragua have each adopted a new legislative framework that requires them to produce a debt management strategy as well as an annual debt report, but they do not require the authorities to publish the debt management strategy. While Croatia and Nicaragua have not yet formulated a debt management strategy, Indonesia has taken a first step, with the minister signing off on the new strategy and making it publicly available as a ministerial decree. Sri Lanka published for the first time in 2004 a debt management report containing information on institutional arrangements, the debt profile, risk indicators, and debt market developments.[12]

Croatia has made significant advances in improving auditing capacity because it is a requirement for entry into the European Union. An internal audit department was set up to monitor internal control of the DMS and will report directly to the finance minister. The Colombian authorities are discussing the need to create a specialized auditing unit to supervise debt management operations that transform the debt profile (for example, through the use of derivatives). Both the comptroller and internal audit are seen as having gaps in specific technical knowledge and understanding of these transactions. The Auditor General in Zambia now produces an annual report on the accounts of the government within the legal period allowed.

In Colombia, the debt office has spent considerable resources and time developing a procedures manual. High staff rotation lends itself to a higher incidence of operational risk. In Indonesia, a detailed review of processes and procedures is to be conducted by an international audit firm as part of the establishment of the new Directorate General for Debt Management. This will provide the basis for preparing procedures manuals for the new directorate general, as well as a code of conduct for staff involved in debt management. In Kenya, the reform plan included drafting organizational guidelines clarifying the responsibilities of the separate units of the debt office and determining the decision-making power within the debt office. In Croatia, designing formal procedures and responsibilities describing organizational guidelines for the DMO showing its internal division of responsibilities and delegation of decision-making power was a priority.

Sri Lanka has taken steps to improve processes and internal procedures for reducing operational risk. The central bank's Public Debt Department (PDD) established a number of mechanisms to manage operational risks, including a detailed procedures manual for all operations, which is readily available and updated regularly. The PDD also had a backup facility to conduct auctions at a remote site. Colombia also implemented actions to reduce operational risk by creating an inventory of and better physical security for all the legal contracts of issued bonds, as well as by introducing an enhanced database with updated information on outstanding bonds.[13]

In Lebanon, the continuous improvement in processes at the PDD provided assurance about the accuracy of payments and recordkeeping. In addition, procedures for borrowing in international capital markets were well documented. Going forward, the authorities plan to streamline the processes further to improve efficiency, produce better documentation, and reduce key-person risk. While some processes were documented, PDD staff continued to rely heavily on the institutional knowledge of experienced staff.

CONCLUSIONS AND INSIGHTS

Most pilot-program countries met the minimum requirement of having legislation that clarified the authority to borrow in the name of the government. This authority, however, was typically found in a number of separate laws introduced for borrowing from different sources at different times. This accretion of legislation, often over many decades, mandated responsibilities for debt management to a number of different entities. It also specified different processes and levels of authority for borrowing (for example, some borrowing requires parliamentary approval while other borrowing can be approved at the level of officials). While most countries get by, these arrangements are frequently inefficient and sometimes require inventive maneuvering for the system to function.

The institutional and political difficulties associated with legislative change frequently hampered the formulation of new laws and amendments. In some cases, a constitutional amendment was required to develop a consistent approach to borrowing. Nevertheless, three pilot countries have succeeded in consolidating legislation in new budget or debt laws. Other pilot countries developed reform programs that avoid legislative change in the early stages and have used secondary regulations (decrees, regulations, and ministerial authority) to implement more urgent initiatives.

Management of public debt in the 12 pilot countries was split across a number of different departments, typically spanning ministries of finance, central banks, and economics and planning ministries. The dispersion of responsibility tended to reflect the source of the borrowing. Changes in institutional responsibilities were frequently recommended to move debt management closer to sound practices, but these changes have proven difficult to implement.

In response to the difficulties of organizational change, one approach was to create a new entity to provide the missing functionality—usually a group to develop a debt management strategy—and to coordinate the work of other debt management entities. Experience with this approach has not been encouraging, however, because it adds a further layer to an already complex set of arrangements.

Another approach was to seek greater cooperation among the different debt managers to make existing institutional arrangements work better. This ranged from the creation of formal coordinating committees to more task-oriented groups, comprising staff drawn from different departments. Such an approach can work well as long as the will is there, or until a particular task is completed, but it is unlikely to be a lasting solution. Indeed, several pilot countries had remnants of coordinating committees that had not met for years, legacies of previous reform efforts.

Improving the quality of disclosure on public debt management was a reasonably straightforward reform. Disclosure could be undertaken on a gradual basis, requiring no legislative change, and the cost of information dissemination via the Internet was comparatively low. However, such improvements were more likely to occur if there was a demand for the information, whether external or internal. External sources of demand included international financial institutions, rating agencies, and investors (given the increasing interest by the international investment community in investing in emerging-market securities).

The disclosure requirements imposed by legislation varied widely across the pilot countries and ranged from a need to table policy statements in parliament to no requirements at all. In some countries, financial statements included budget flows only, not stocks of debt, and were produced with delays of up to several years. In others, legislative requirements to produce information were ignored and sanctions were not applied. Improving reporting standards and ensuring they are applied is an issue larger than public debt management, so reforms in this area must be closely coordinated with broader efforts.

Public debt management involves transactions of considerable size and the operational risk can thus be large. These risks grow more extensive and complex as countries move from bilateral and multilateral sources of funding to market-based financing. To manage this, leading DMOs have drawn on sound practices in the financial sector. They have instituted such measures as segregation of responsibilities (including separation of front- and back-office activities), checks and balances in the system, business continuity planning, and stringent ethical guidelines. Reform and capacity-building programs for public debt management need to incorporate the sound management of operational risk in a more systematic manner. The level of awareness and measures adopted in the 12 pilot countries, however, displays only a partial approach to the management of these risks.

A major challenge for achieving accountability has been to obtain adequate independent assurance about reporting and about the processes used by public debt managers. In some countries, the external auditor (usually the "supreme auditor") publicly called for improvements to the management of public debt, including institutional arrangements, the need for a strategy, and better accounting. In others, external audits were confined to financial statements, which had no information about the stock of debt. In all countries, the specialized nature of transactions in financial markets called for an external auditor competent in treasury accounting and able to provide assurances about the risk and control environment in the debt management unit. The supreme audit institution might, however, find it hard to cover this specialty because its operations are more oriented toward the general functions of government. In developing reform programs for public debt management, it is important to consider how external assurance would be provided. This could include hiring external audit firms with the requisite experience to perform periodic reviews.

Capacity: Staff and Debt Management Systems

STAFF CAPACITY

Public debt management requires staff with a combination of financial market, economics, and public policy skills. Regardless of the institutional structure, the ability to attract and retain skilled debt management personnel is crucial, both for developing and executing an effective strategy and for mitigating key-person risk (the risk of expertise residing in only one or two persons).

Diagnostics in Pilot Countries

Building staff capacity is a challenge in many public sector reform programs in developing countries, and experience in public debt management in the pilot countries was no exception. Two common issues were identified: First, in several countries, public sector laws, rules, and practices impeded the recruitment and retention of sufficient staff, or those with the appropriate mix of skills. For example, the law in Lebanon capped public debt department staff at eight, making it more difficult for the department to expand into a full range of functions, such as risk analysis and market borrowing. Recruiting in Croatia, Indonesia (to some degree), and Nicaragua was complicated by the fact that placement of new staff was determined by a central personnel office in the finance ministry, and the head of the debt management unit often did not have the final say on who was hired. Compulsory staff rotation policies can result in turnover that is too rapid—no sooner than staff members are trained, they are rotated to other divisions in the ministry of finance.

Recruitment of skilled staff in the pilot countries was also complicated by the low salaries paid at the finance ministries. In Bulgaria, Costa Rica, Croatia, Kenya, Lebanon, Nicaragua, and Tunisia, the salary differentials between the finance ministry and the central bank, as well as the private sector, were an issue.

Second, high staff turnover was a problem in Colombia, Croatia, and Kenya. As staff gained skills and experience in public debt management, they became attractive to the private sector. In Kenya, the Swedish International Development Cooperation Agency (SIDA), with technical support from the Swedish National Debt Office, helped build capacity in the debt management unit over a 10-year period, yet those staff members who were well trained left for more lucrative jobs.[1] In Colombia, to overcome budgetary constraints in the ministry of finance, external consultants were hired whose salaries were paid by projects financed with external assistance. However, these consultants left after gaining experience with international capital market placements and derivatives, and without passing on their acquired skills to ministry staff.

Apart from low compensation for technical skills, a paucity of training opportunities and inadequate budgets for training also hindered staff retention. Budget constraints in Costa Rica, Kenya, Nicaragua, and Zambia meant that there were no formal training programs for staff working on debt management.

Action Plans and Reform Experiences

The pilot countries addressed the challenges in building staff capacity in public debt management through various channels, including

- on-the-job training and short-term external assignments;
- improved incentives for career progression;
- use of existing public sector capacity-building programs and international support networks;
- use of resident advisors, external consultants, and secondments from the central bank;
- relaxation of human resources management restrictions; and
- establishment of islands of excellence or enclaves.

Those pilot countries able to recruit university graduates eager to learn the profession and wanting to contribute to public service, but lacking specialized knowledge, emphasized on-the-job-training, improved incentives for career progression, and provision of exciting job opportunities (Bulgaria, Colombia, Croatia, Indonesia, Lebanon, and Sri Lanka).

Short-term external assignments were also used as incentives to upgrade capacity. These assignments were mostly with investment banks, but were only available for debt management staff in middle-income countries that issue international bonds. For example, staff from Colombia's debt management office received job training at an investment bank in New York. Study tours to Organisation for Economic Co-operation and Development debt offices were also valuable. For example, Sri Lankan officials visited the Swedish National Debt Office, and officials from Colombia visited debt management offices in a number of countries. More extensive interaction with officials in other countries can be achieved through twinning arrangements, which have been used in Bulgaria and Sri Lanka.

Several pilot countries made active use of capacity-building institutions and programs for the general public sector. For example, Lebanon and Sri Lanka have well-established training and capacity-building programs to upgrade and maintain the skills of all staff in the organization. In Bulgaria, the Public Finance School—financed by the European Union and established in Sofia in 2004—offers training courses to finance ministry staff. Colombia had an arrangement with a local university that offered general training in public debt management to debt managers and auditors.[2]

For small economies, establishing such a school or institution can be expensive relative to narrow domestic demand. Economies of scale can be obtained if training and skills upgrading are obtained through such regional capacity-building institutions as the Macroeconomic and Financial Management Institute of Eastern and Southern Africa (MEFMI; box 6.1), the West African Institute for Financial and Economic Management, the Regional Debt Management Training Unit for Central Africa and Western Africa, *Centro de Estudios Monetarios Latinoamericanos*, and the Center for Excellence in Slovenia.

Pilot-program countries also boosted organizational capacity by using resident advisors, secondments, and external consultants. For example, Bulgaria, Indonesia, Nicaragua, Sri Lanka, and Zambia hosted resident advisors financed by the U.S. Treasury and by the United Nations Development Programme in Lebanon and Tunisia. Secondments from the central bank were used in Kenya, Nicaragua, and Sri Lanka. In Kenya, the reform plan in the finance ministry stalled until the central bank seconded two senior staff to the ministry's Debt Management Department

BOX 6.1 | **Capacity Building through the Macroeconomic and Financial Management Institute of Eastern and Southern Africa**

In December 1992, a steering group of central bank governors and permanent secretaries from finance ministries from 12 eastern and southern African countries met (at a workshop organized by the World Bank and the United Nations Development Programme (UNDP)) to consider alternative approaches to traditional country-by-country debt management training programs. These traditional programs consisted mainly of courses typically conducted outside the region, short missions, and duplicative donor-supported programs that did not fully address the needs of senior economic managers. They were insufficiently focused on institutional, organizational, and human resources problems.

MEFMI was set up to counteract this traditional approach, and is based on a regional initiative to deliver quality services to member countries and develop—and assist in implementing—comprehensive capacity-building programs. It became a regional center offering new training products and services, while also serving as a focal point for coordinating the technical assistance efforts of international agencies and ensuring that the activities developed are tailored to the specific requirements of the region. These needs include macroeconomic management, financial sector management, debt management, and multidisciplinary activities programs

MEFMI coordinates the division of labor with the other agencies.[a] The World Bank's Development Economics Data Group provides training in debt sustainability analysis, the United Nations Conference on Trade and Development and the Commonwealth Secretariat provide training in debt recording systems, the International Monetary Fund and the African Development Bank offer training in macroeconomic management, and the Bank for International Settlements and the Federal Reserve Bank of New York offer courses in financial sector management.

Source: www.mefmi.org.

a. MEFMI is financially supported by the African Capacity Building Foundation and by the governments of Denmark, the Netherlands, Sweden, and Switzerland. It is supported technically by the World Bank, the IMF, the Bank for International Settlements, the African Development Bank, the Commonwealth Secretariat, United Nations Conference on Trade and Development, United Nations Institute for Training and Research, the Federal Reserve Bank of New York, and Debt Relief International.

(DMD). These staff members now constitute the management team of the DMD and one is the project team leader of the pilot program.

In Kenya, Pakistan, Sri Lanka, and Zambia, the skills shortages in finance ministries contributed to the transfer of at least some debt management functions to the central bank, where the necessary skills existed and staff retention was better. In contrast to secondments, which can help build capacity in the finance ministry, know-how is not transferred when debt management functions are carried out in the central bank. Therefore, this can only be a temporary solution to the long-term challenge of building capacity in the finance ministry.[3]

Pilot countries also used external consultants for advice on specific issues. For example, Indonesia engaged a number of external consultants under an Australian Agency for International Development (AusAID) program to help it address such issues as systems control and procedures, risk management reporting, and information technology.

The use of outside advisors under long-term arrangements allows countries to build effective working relationships and monitor progress on a continuous basis. However, such advisors do not necessarily transfer skills to permanent staff, with the risk that when the assignments end, the organization reverts to its former operations. This risk can be mitigated by having the terms of reference stress the importance of building the capacity of staff. Another risk with long-term arrangements is that the skill base of the advisor might not extend to all the required areas; this, however, can be remedied by close supervision of the consultant by an executive agency that has a good understanding of the substance (box 6.2).

One short-run effort to fill skill gaps among operational staff in some pilot-program countries has been for special advisors and ministers to do the job themselves, rather than delegate important debt management functions to ministry staff. This occurred particularly with front-office functions, such as issuing bonds in international markets (Bulgaria, Croatia, and Lebanon). This might, however, heighten key-person risk; parallel efforts to build staff capacity are still necessary.

Lebanon has taken a two-pronged approach to developing capacity. First, it is gradually strengthening the permanent finance ministry department, although, as noted earlier, there are constraints on the extent to which specialized professional skills can be developed. In parallel, to compensate for the slow buildup of capacity in the ministry, a separate unit, assisted by a donor agency, was set up to provide further specialized capacity, mainly for front- and middle-office tasks.[4] While the two units perform different functions, the specialized unit is also tasked with building capacity in the ministry.

In Indonesia, a new department was set up in 2000 to manage domestic borrowing—a function not required before the financial crisis in the late 1990s. This department received considerable capacity-building support from AusAID.[5] The department also enjoyed special treatment within the ministry through improved career progression opportunities, flexibility in the application of public sector pay scales and rotation schemes, better information technology resources, access to international training, and exciting work. Career opportunities also provided staff with a sense of mission, with the result that staff turnover has been low.

BOX 6.2 | **Building Debt Management Capacity in Kenya: Experience of the Swedish Agency for International Development Cooperation (SIDA)**

A reform project to upgrade public debt management in Kenya was implemented and documented in a SIDA evaluation report for the period 1986–96. The initial phase of the project was supported by a joint World Bank–UNDP–SIDA effort, the second phase was supported solely by SIDA, and the third phase had no outside support.

One of the main problems encountered during the project was that gains in strengthening the capacity and quality of public debt management were lost very quickly. A Debt Management Division (DMD) in the finance ministry was established and initially enjoyed strong support from senior management in the finance ministry, particularly from the permanent secretary. But by 1993, most of the senior management members who supported the project left the ministry. In addition, during 1994–2005, the best-trained staff departed as a result of the low salaries and limited career development prospects in the ministry and their increased attractiveness to the private sector. This weakened the ministry's capacity to carry on such tasks as improving the accuracy of debt recording and drafting debt management reports. The SIDA report indicated that by 1997, capacity in the DMD had regressed to its level of five years earlier.

As a consequence, debt management was given increasingly less priority in the overall macroeconomic management of the finance ministry. The downgrading of the importance of debt management can be explained partly by the less precarious debt service situation in Kenya following the recovery of the economy and the completion of negotiations with the Paris Club of official creditors.

The lessening priority of debt management was evident in the authorities' unwillingness to upgrade the reporting line for debt management. The DMD was placed under the Fiscal and Monetary Affairs Department. The World Bank and UNDP, in their evaluation of the finance ministry's 1994 report, "highly recommended" stronger efforts in the field of debt management by establishing a separate Public Debt Department within the ministry. Having the DMD report directly to the finance secretary would have fortified its role.

Setting up such separate units to create "islands of excellence" has succeeded in building capacity, but it has added to fragmented institutional arrangements with the attendant challenges (described in chapter 3). An added risk of this approach is its potential to distort the government's capacity-building efforts in the overall public sector (by draining skills from core ministries or reducing incentives for broader-based reforms). Indonesia and Lebanon have addressed these issues; over the medium term, they have plans to merge the specialized units into consolidated debt offices within the finance ministries.

In Tunisia, a "corps" established for particular professional capacities within the public sector enjoys better remuneration, including acceler-

Box 6.2 *continued*

Strengthening the capacity of debt management was complicated in that assistance to build capacity was centered on the DMD, although three different departments were responsible for different aspects of public debt management. The Kenyan central bank was also involved in domestic debt management. The task of dealing with domestic debt was given to the DMD, but it was deemed to be unprepared to assume that responsibility. In the early 1990s, the central bank had proposed taking over the entire debt management function from the finance ministry but this did not happen.

The SIDA report suggested that "the multitude of different units involved in Kenya's debt management was administratively cumbersome and difficult to handle in practice. By necessity the cooperation was complicated by internal rivalries and/or lack of cooperation, and even by the sheer work effort required to cooperate with and pass on information to others" (SIDA 1996).

Finally, the authorities agreed to help establish and strengthen the role of committees but this effort also came to a halt in the face of reduced priority for debt management issues. A Debt Management Committee (DMC) was established, chaired by the Permanent Secretary of the ministry of finance. Its task was to analyze recommendations by the Debt Management Technical Working Group and advise on matters related to the management of government external and domestic debt. The working group was chaired by the head of the DMD. Both the DMC and the working group were reportedly meeting almost every month. However, the activity and importance of these organizations seem to have declined, especially after 1994.

One of the main lessons of the SIDA report was the importance of embedding the DMD institutionally by establishing clearer routines, handbooks for debt recording and debt management, and a stronger internal position within the finance ministry. Also, countermeasures such as offering extra benefits to particularly talented staff, bonding, some topping up, and establishing clear career progression may have helped to at least delay the almost simultaneous departure of many of the staff.

Source: SIDA 1996.

ated promotions, bonuses, and a separate occupational scale. Although this arrangement has not been applied to staff in debt management, it is an option for the authorities to consider. Nicaragua is implementing a broader reform with a new civil service law that enables the government to rationalize and improve remuneration for skilled staff. It has selected a firm to evaluate functions and salaries in the public sector. In Kenya, similar reforms are planned at the finance ministry, in coordination with the civil service reform secretariat responsible for the reform of the broader public sector.

In pilot-program countries with little flexibility in civil service employment structures, such measures can be hard to implement. These countries may be under pressure to set up debt management agencies outside the rigid civil service system. In Pakistan, one of the main reasons for establishing the Debt Policy Coordination Office was that it would be able to pay market salaries outside the civil service structure. The Sri Lankan authorities' desire was to take debt management responsibilities out of the central bank. Weaknesses in the finance ministry, however, led to discussion of establishing a separate agency, but a subsequent government decided against it. The Bulgarian government also considered taking debt management responsibilities out of the ministry of finance but it too decided against it.[6]

DEBT MANAGEMENT SYSTEMS

Debt management activities should be supported by accurate and comprehensive information technology (IT) systems that are properly safeguarded. Countries seeking to build capacity in government debt management should assign high priority to developing accurate debt recording and reporting systems to ensure timely payment of debt service and to produce consolidated debt data. IT systems are also necessary for undertaking scenario analyses and for improving the quality of budgetary reporting and the transparency of government financial accounts. The authorities should be able to independently verify requests for payments sent by creditors.

Diagnostics in Pilot Countries

Most of the pilot countries had debt recording systems that supported the timely payment of debt service. However, in Zambia, the external debt database was incomplete. In Pakistan, despite significant efforts to establish an accurate and up-to-date database, a general mistrust of the data in the system persisted and the debt service unit kept manual files on every outstanding loan, against which creditor payment notices were checked.

One of the main IT systems problems observed in the pilot countries was that public debt was recorded on more than one system. (Table 6.1 summarizes the debt-recording systems used—for external and domestic debt—at the time of the diagnostic missions.) Multiple systems can make it difficult to undertake tasks that require data on the entire portfolio, such as forecasting cash flow, producing consolidated reports on total debt, and performing analysis that supports strategy development (scenario analysis, for example). Multiple systems were seen in Indonesia, Kenya, Lebanon, Pakistan, Sri Lanka, and Tunisia.

While manual workarounds were performed in these countries, such as downloading to Microsoft Excel or Microsoft Access, the task could be cumbersome, because the output from the databases was not uniform.[7] In Indonesia, analysis was conducted on Microsoft Excel spreadsheets, but staff typically built their own datasets and did not rely on the debt recording system's database.[8]

TABLE 6.1   Debt-Recording Systems in Pilot-Program Countries

Country	External debt	Domestic debt
Bulgaria	In-house system (including guarantees)	
Colombia	Off-the-shelf system (including guarantees)	
Costa Rica	DMFAS[a]	SATV
Croatia	Off-the-shelf system (including guarantees)	
Indonesia	In-house system based on Microsoft Access for external and domestic securities	
	Duplicate recording in DMFAS (in ministry of finance) and an in-house system (in central bank)[b]	In-house system for domestic securities in the central bank as central registry
Kenya	CS-DRMS (including guarantees and on-lending)[c]	In-house system
Lebanon	DMFAS	In-house system
Nicaragua	DMFAS (including guarantees)	Stand-alone system for central bank debt Stand-alone system for treasury debt A different DMFAS for other domestic debt
Pakistan	DMFAS	Microsoft Excel–based system for government securities Manual system for retail instruments
Sri Lanka	CS-DRMS	Microsoft Access
Tunisia	In-house system (including guarantees)	Microsoft Excel
Zambia	DMFAS (including guarantees)	Microsoft Access

Source: World Bank Treasury staff.
Note: CS-DRMS = Commonwealth Secretariat Debt Recording and Management System; DMFAS = Debt Management Financial and Analysis System; SATV = Sistema de Administración de Títulos Valores.
a. DMFAS is run by UNCTAD. UNCTAD activities cover the installation of DMFAS, as well as training and assistance in its use, particularly to enable debt officers to establish a complete and up-to-date debt database and to provide timely and accurate debt statistics. Activities also include maintenance and system support and advice on institutional and procedural issues. For more information, see http://r0.unctad.org/dmfas/.
b. Central bank in-house system has been migrated to its own installation of DMFAS.
c. CS-DRMS is run by the Commonwealth Secretariat, which helps countries record, analyze, and manage the debt. For more information, see http://www.csdrms.org/.

The fragmentation of databases reflected institutional arrangements in which different components of the debt were managed by different offices and institutions. Thus, synergies were not exploited because recording and servicing domestic and external debt essentially involve the same skills and technology. Only Bulgaria, Colombia, and Croatia recorded external and domestic debt in one system; they were also the only pilot countries with consolidated central government debt management units.[9]

Database fragmentation might also reflect the evolution of the public debt and its systems providers. External debt has been a more significant burden for developing countries than domestic debt and it therefore received more attention from the international community. As a result, external debt data recorded in CS-DRMS and DMFAS have long histories and are of comparatively good quality because the systems responded to the demand of the international financial institutions for good data.[10] Only the latest versions of the CS-DRMS and DMFAS systems allow the recording of domestic debt, so most countries that used these systems had to develop or purchase alternative systems to record domestic debt.

Separate databases could also cause complications when recording swap transactions between foreign-currency and domestic-currency debt. The two countries that have carried out such transactions—Bulgaria and Colombia—had unified databases and therefore did not face this problem.[11] Also, "traditional" debt management systems, such as CS-DRMS and DMFAS, do not currently handle swaps easily, and some type of workaround is required.

Efficiency gains, improved quality of budgetary reporting, and transparency of government financial accounts can also be achieved when debt management systems are able to interface with the rest of the public sector financial systems (accounting and budget execution, for example). Most of the countries in the pilot program, however, had no electronic interface. For example, in Lebanon, although DMFAS has the capacity, it was not integrated with the finance ministry's overall financial management systems, which themselves consisted of a series of modules with limited integration.[12] In Croatia, the debt recording system used at the time of the diagnostics was a modular system that could be linked to other systems, but the financial management system did not allow for interface. As a consequence, the data from the system relating to debt service payments had to be manually reentered into the public financial management system for budget execution purposes.

Supplier risk was noted in Croatia, where ongoing systems support was not provided, in part because of delays in license payments by the finance ministry. Risk also lay in the fact that Croatia was only the debt management system vendor's second customer and it was unclear whether the vendor was willing to support the system in the future. In addition, the vendor did not have support staff in Zagreb that could help in the event of a system failure, which, given the system's age, was increasingly likely.[13] Colombia also lacked system vendor support and was approaching capacity limits. This vulnerability was made clear when the system failed in early 2001, prompting the government to seriously consider upgrading the debt management system.

Action Plans and Reform Experiences

Actions taken to upgrade debt management systems among the pilot countries included

- improving debt recording capacity,
- producing consolidated debt reporting,
- securing debt databases and IT systems, and
- integrating debt recording with the public financial management system.

Because the quality of the debt database has been a continuing concern, improved debt recording received the highest priority in several pilot-country reform programs. Reforms to improve the quality of the database have been ongoing in Pakistan, and this continues to be a key area for reform implementation. Similarly, in Zambia, after some setbacks in its ability to maintain the quality of data, the authorities made debt recording a priority. The government trained 20 staff in the DMFAS system and, following an examination, selected 11 qualified staff to work in the back office with a mandate to reconcile the database.

In Nicaragua, improvements addressing the inefficient use of resources arising from the duplication of debt recording are under way. The central bank and the ministry of finance embarked on a project allowing the finance ministry to have read-only access to DMFAS records on external debt in the central bank. This will allow the parallel work carried out in the finance ministry to keep track of the external debt stock to be discontinued.

One of the key objectives for consolidating systems is to enable debt managers to produce consolidated debt reporting on the status of the total debt stock and to conduct forward-looking analysis. Several approaches were observed in the pilot countries. The first and most comprehensive approach was to undertake a full review of IT requirements following reforms to institutional arrangements and associated business processes. This approach was implemented in Croatia, where the liquidity management function was moved from the Budget Execution Section to the Debt Management Section in the finance ministry. Based on a thorough user requirements analysis, the government decided that a new debt management system should be installed. In Colombia, by contrast, the merger between treasury cash management functions and the debt management office took place while parallel work on system reform was already under way, but these reforms were not closely coordinated.

The second approach was to proceed with short-term solutions to "bridge" the existing information systems (Costa Rica, Indonesia, and Lebanon). The short-term objective in these countries was to ensure that staff had easy access to updated information on outstanding debt and related future cash flows, using existing debt recording systems. This involved downloading information from the respective systems and producing a new database with the overall debt data on a spreadsheet.

A longer-term IT strategy should study whether the best solution is automating the consolidation process through a "consolidator" system, having existing systems function as the overall debt recording system via links between existing systems (if possible), or establishing a centralized database. In Kenya and Sri Lanka, efforts to create comprehensive debt databases are being implemented through the installation of the domestic debt module in CS-DRMS 2000+. In Tunisia, efforts to consolidate the IT system have been under way on the external debt side; the central bank and the finance ministry have sponsored the development of a centralized database (known as SIADE) that has a modern, open architecture design and is supported by a dedicated team of system specialists.

Weaknesses in debt management systems were the result of senior management paying little attention to system implementation projects and end users rarely being involved in the design and implementation phase. For example, in Croatia, in the buildup of the SAP's (Systems Applications and Products in Data Processing) debt management module, the project was managed by an IT-dominated implementation team. No finance ministry steering committee was overseeing the process and few end users were involved in the project. The absence of a steering committee to oversee the implementation and to make decisions on the direction of the implementation process was presumably one of the reasons why the SAP's debt management module has not been operational, because users' views were not adequately reflected in the decision-making process. Investing in systems is expensive, not only for the initial investment, but for operating costs as well. Thus, mistakes need to be minimized and a holistic view of debt management system needs is necessary.[14]

Securing the debt database and IT systems has been a priority in Colombia, Croatia, and Sri Lanka. In Sri Lanka, the central bank had endured a bombing; as a result, the government had taken steps to create a backup facility for storing records and made a weekly backup of all data to tape, which was stored externally. The new central depository system has real-time backup at a remote site and will enhance the security of its debt database.

Integrating debt recording systems with the rest of the public financial management system to improve efficiency and reduce operational risk by reducing the need for duplicate data input has been a challenge. None of the pilot countries have achieved such integration, although some have attempted or are attempting to do so. One approach was to create a single integrated treasury management system encompassing all aspects of public financial management, including debt management; this was the intent of the SAP system introduced in Croatia. In Colombia, the effort to link debt recording with the rest of the public financial management system has taken the form of participating in a broader IT reform in the public sector (box 6.3).

Another approach has been to link the debt recording system with the public financial management system. Nicaragua has been trying to create an automated interface between the debt recording systems in the public credit office and the accounting system. The goal is to alleviate the duplication of data entry into both and to reduce the possibility for error attributable to the level of manual intervention. In Bulgaria, the EU is assisting the Budget Directorate to create a financial management information system. With that in place, the plan is to electronically link the existing debt management system.

CONCLUSIONS AND INSIGHTS

The recruitment and retention of skilled and experienced staff is one of the greatest challenges for improving the quality of public debt management in most pilot-program countries. Unless this need is addressed, significant efforts by governments and donors will have, at best, only a transitory impact. The nature and combination of the problems vary across countries, but include insufficient staff numbers, staff with the wrong skills mix, high turnover, excessive rotation of staff in the finance ministry, inadequate training budgets, and a lack of training opportunities. While budgetary

BOX 6.3   **IT Reform Experience in Colombia**

In 2002, Colombian authorities created a centralized IT General Directorate in the finance ministry and abolished, simultaneously, the multiple decentralized IT offices—one for each of the five ministry directorates, including the general public credit directorate.

The rationale was that, under the previous arrangement, the different IT functions were fragmented and inefficient, with 72 servers, 86 applications, and multiple technology bases. A more specific objective was to migrate from a client-server environment to an Internet computing environment, with full integration of software and related facilities. Because the IT framework was not integrated, differences in finance ministry data frequently arose, impairing decision making.

This change in orientation and organizational support has significant implications for all ministry IT processes, including those of public debt management. The Debt Directorate welcomed the change because it had already decided that its IT and debt management software needed a complete overhaul. The main deficiencies were shortcomings in the quality of the database, and the fact that the existing system was outdated; it ultimately collapsed in early 2001, and even though it was quickly restored, the incident underscored the urgent need for change.

The authorities initially planned to acquire DMFAS software supplied by UNCTAD. In the process, the finance ministry requested that the DMFAS be integrated with Internet computing but the software could not meet this requirement. This had especially significant implications for debt registration and monitoring of subnational debt. Another difficulty with DMFAS was that it would take two years to fully develop and install the software.

Instead of buying DMFAS, the authorities chose to develop the software in the ministry, taking advantage of the new IT Directorate, and migrated to an Oracle database. If successful, this move will simplify back-office processes, allow better quality data, facilitate the analytical work of the middle office, and make debt management operations more transparent.[a]

Source: Ministry of Finance of Colombia and World Bank Treasury staff.
a. An IT audit will be necessary to determine the new system's success.

issues within finance ministries underlie a number of these problems, poor management of staff and the low priority given to the function within the ministries are also factors. These problems, of course, are not unique to public debt management. They affect many other core functions within finance ministries and other parts of government. First-best solutions must, therefore, focus on improving the quality of government services in general. However, this will likely be a long-term endeavor for countries afflicted with corruption, poor governance, and little tradition of quality in government.

In these circumstances, some countries have opted for variations on the islands-of-excellence model, insulating the debt management function from the resource constraints faced elsewhere in government. Pilot countries have also explored the possibility of establishing public debt management offices separate from finance ministries.[15] This approach has not been adopted in any of the pilot countries because they were concerned about a number of disadvantages, particularly the need to coordinate public debt management with other core policy functions.

To address staff capacity issues, pilot countries are using a variety of measures permitted by their institutional frameworks. For staff development, these include individual career plans for each staff member and access to local and world-class training opportunities with the help of donors (academic and vocational courses, and on-the-job placements). Retention can be improved by making full use of the existing flexibility for remuneration policy, including accelerated promotion, bonuses, or separate occupational pay scales, as well as exempting staff from ministry rotation policies. The skill base of debt management units can be supplemented by hiring staff on fixed-term assignments, particularly when a new organization is being established or a significant expansion of capacity is implemented.[16] Although well-qualified graduates with the core skills for higher-level analysis might be available for recruitment, countries also need a core of more experienced personnel to train and mentor them. Other measures to build staff capacity can be more subtle, such as improving the physical and IT environments and creating a strong sense of mission and identity for the department.

Although the various means of capacity building each has its strengths and drawbacks, country authorities must develop capacity-building programs that meet their specific needs, rather than those that simply accept training offered by donors or other free training.

The need for sound debt recording systems has long been recognized and has been the focus of considerable development assistance by many donors. Despite this, a few pilot countries still struggle with basic debt recording and reporting. The main problems usually relate to inadequate processes and procedures guiding the debt management transactions, and the failure to use the full capabilities of the IT system. A more common challenge is the integration of data from separate systems; domestic debt is usually recorded in a separate system from the external debt recording system, reflecting separate institutional arrangements. Although this is not insurmountable, the workarounds required can be slow and entail double entry of data, which increases operational risk. As a result, a complete picture of a country's debt can be difficult to obtain and the ability to extract data for analysis might be impeded. Finally, as countries gain market access and use a broader array of instruments (such as swaps), their needs frequently exceed the capabilities of their systems.

Ideally, the development of IT systems should reflect reforms of institutional arrangements and the functions of debt management units. User requirements after such reforms can differ substantively from before and, indeed, the reform process itself provides the opportunity to improve the efficiency of business processes. Locking in to particular IT systems before completing these stages raises the risk that the systems will not deliver what the organization needs. A reform program that is centered only on a major IT acquisition and that does not give sufficient attention to having proper and robust business processes is unlikely to succeed, as the objective becomes getting the system in place rather than improving all public debt management outputs.

Rather than embark on major systems projects, a number of countries in the pilot program decided to improve IT systems by taking smaller steps such as making better use of existing systems (recording domestic debt in the external debt system, for example) and developing better interfaces to produce more easily consolidated debt reporting outputs. This approach has the advantage of producing faster results and allowing time to better assess longer-term needs, which may be contingent upon other development efforts yet to be specified.

APPENDIX

TABLE A.1 Summary of Legislative Framework in Public Debt Management in the 12 Pilot Countries

Country	Delegation of authority	Overall debt limit	Limits on guarantees	Annual borrowing limits; Annual limits on guarantees	Limit on borrowing by other public sector entities	Approval of external debt by parliament	Objective for debt management	Functions of government units	Requirement to determine strategy
Bulgaria	State Budget Act (delegated to Council of Ministers) and Law on Government Debt (from COM to Minister of Finance)	Law on Government Debt	Law on Government Debt	Law on Government Debt; Law on Government Debt		National Assembly approves all foreign transactions	Debt Management Strategy Document		Law on Government Debt
Colombia	Law 533 and Decree 2681	Resolution 2681			Law 550	Resolution 2681		Decree 771/01	
Costa Rica	General Debt Law	External Debt Law Law 7671 Law 7970		Annual Budget Law; none	General Debt Law	General Debt Law superseded by External Debt Law			

(continued)

Croatia	Budget Act (to the full government)	Budget Act		Budget Execution Act	Budget Act	Budget Act	Regulation on the internal structure of the finance ministry	Budget Act
Indonesia	Government Securities Law for securities and Treasury Law for loans	State Finance Law (2003)		Annual Budget Law	State Finance Law	Budget Act For loans from international financial institutions, Law on International Agreements and Contracts	Ministerial Decree	
Kenya	Internal Loans Act and the External Loans and Credits Act	Limits on external debt but no limits on domestic debt	Guarantee (Loans) Act	No limits on domestic debt		None	Government Regulation	None
Lebanon	Constitution vests the Treasury as the principal debt manager; Establishment law of CDR allows CDR to source foreign currency debt on behalf of the government			Annual Budget Law	Prohibited	A law for each loan	Law 10092 Administrative Law	None

TABLE A.1 *continued*

Country	Delegation of authority	Overall debt limit	Limits on guarantees	Annual borrowing limits; Annual limits on guarantees	Limit on borrowing by other public sector entities	Approval of external debt by parliament	Objective for debt management	Functions of government units	Requirement to determine strategy
Nicaragua	Public Debt Law	Public Debt Law			General Budget Law		Public Debt Law	Secondary legislation	
Pakistan	Pakistani Constitution and Rules of Business (ordinance passed that distributes responsibility to each unit within the government)	Fiscal Responsibility and Debt Limitation Act	Fiscal Responsibility and Debt Limitation Act	Fiscal Responsibility and Debt Limitation Act		n.a.	None	Government Regulation	Fiscal Responsibility and Debt Limitation Act
Sri Lanka	Monetary Law Act Local Treasury Bills Ordinance Registered Stock and Securities Ordinance Foreign Loans Act Treasury Certificate of Deposit Act	Fiscal Management (Responsibility) Act (2002)		Annual Appropriation Act				None	None

Country				
Tunisia	Annual Law of Finance; Annual Law of Finance	Code of Public Accounting	Constitution	None
Zambia	Loans and Guarantees Act, Bretton Woods Agreement Act, IDA Act, General Loans Act and the Development Bond Act	Loans and Guarantees Act	Loans and guarantees (maximum amounts) Orders	

Source: World Bank Treasury staff.
Note: n.a. = Not applicable.

TABLE A.2   Distribution of Debt Management Functions

Country	Location of front-office functions				Location of back-office functions		
	Unit 1	*Unit 2*	*Unit 3*	*Unit 4*	*Unit 1*	*Unit 2*	*Unit 3*
Bulgaria	State debt directorate in ministry of finance responsible for domestic and foreign debt	Budget execution office responsible for cash management bills			State debt directorate in ministry of finance responsible for all government debt	Budget execution office responsible for cash management bills	
Colombia	Directorate of Public Credit responsible for external and domestic debt	Treasury responsible for shorter-dated debt			Directorate of Public Credit responsible for all debt		
Costa Rica	Treasury responsible for domestic and external debt issued by the government	Central bank responsible for domestic and external debt issued by the central bank			Treasury responsible for domestic and external debt issued by the government	Central bank responsible for domestic and external debt issued by the central bank	

Croatia	Debt Management Sector responsible for domestic and external marketable debt	International Financial Institutions Department responsible for multilateral loans	Budget Execution Sector responsible for cash management bills[a]	Debt Management Sector responsible for domestic and external marketable debt	International Financial Institutions Department responsible for multilateral loans	Budget Execution Sector responsible for cash management bills
Indonesia	DPSUN in Treasury responsible for marketable domestic and foreign debt	External Funds Department in Treasury responsible for bilateral and multilateral loans		DPSUN in Treasury responsible for domestic and foreign securities debt	External Funds Department in Treasury responsible for external loans	Unit in central bank responsible for external loans (duplicate of Unit 2)
Kenya	Ministry of finance responsible for foreign debt	Central bank responsible for domestic debt		Ministry of finance responsible for foreign debt	Central bank responsible for domestic debt	
Lebanon	Public debt department	Council for Reconstruction and Development responsible for multilateral and bilateral loans	Central bank responsible for management of auctions for domestic debt	Ministry of finance responsible for external debt	Central bank responsible for domestic and external debt payments and recording	

(continued)

TABLE A.2 *continued*

	Location of front-office functions				Location of back-office functions		
Country	*Unit 1*	*Unit 2*	*Unit 3*	*Unit 4*	*Unit 1*	*Unit 2*	*Unit 3*
Nicaragua	Treasury responsible for restructured debt	Ministry of finance responsible for domestic debt	Central bank responsible for domestic and external debt		Treasury responsible for restructured debt	Ministry of finance responsible for domestic debt	Central bank responsible for domestic and external debt
Pakistan	Unit in ministry of finance responsible for foreign debt contracted from official creditors	Unit in ministry of finance responsible for foreign debt raised in the international capital markets	Central bank responsible for marketable domestic debt	Central Directorate of National Savings responsible for domestic retail borrowing	Unit in ministry of finance responsible for foreign debt	Unit in central bank responsible for domestic debt	Central Directorate of National Savings responsible for retail borrowing
Sri Lanka	Ministry of Policy Development and Implementation responsible for official borrowing and grants	Central bank responsible for domestic debt	General Treasury responsible for loans from state banks and foreign commercial borrowings		Central bank responsible for domestic and external debt		

Tunisia	Ministry of finance responsible for domestic debt and foreign non-marketable commercial debt	Ministry of Development and International Cooperation responsible for multilateral debt	Ministry of Foreign Affairs responsible for bilateral financing of projects	Central bank responsible for foreign marketable debt	Ministry of finance responsible for domestic and external debt	
Zambia	Ministry of finance responsible for foreign debt	Central bank responsible for domestic debt			Ministry of finance responsible for external debt	Central bank responsible for domestic debt

Source: World Bank Treasury staff.

Note: n.a. = Not applicable.

a. Following recommendation in the Assessment Report, this function has now been moved to the Debt Management Sector.

NOTES

CHAPTER 1

1. IMF 2005a. See also IMF (2006a).
2. The World Bank has been responsible for most of the work.
3. The first assessment missions took place between 2002 and 2004: Bulgaria, June 2002; Colombia, November 2002; Costa Rica, 2003; Croatia, February 2004; Indonesia, April 2004; Kenya, January 2004; Lebanon, December 2003; Nicaragua, January 2004; Pakistan, November 2004; Sri Lanka, October 2002; Tunisia, May 2004; and Zambia, May 2004.
4. Several individual country case studies will be made available on the World Bank Web site as well as on the Web sites of the relevant country authorities.
5. These include reform experiences and initiatives that predate the pilot program that can be useful for other countries attempting to implement reforms.

CHAPTER 2

1. Procrastination on fiscal adjustment, coupled with pressures on debt managers to reduce short-term costs, probably led to more severe crises than if action had been taken earlier (see, for example, Dornbush (2001), Frankel and Wei (2005)).
2. This could also help reduce inflation.
3. For details, see box 5.2.
4. This is described in detail in *Developing the Domestic Government Debt Market*, the companion volume to *Managing Public Debt: From Diagnostics to Reform Implementation*.
5. This was seen in the first round of debt management capacity building in Indonesia early this decade.
6. Samples of the reform plans developed in pilot countries will be published on the Web site http://treasury.worldbank.org/ or government Web sites; for example, for Lebanon's reform plan, see http://www.finance.gov.lb/The+Ministry/Reforms+at+Ministry/Reforms+at+the+Ministry+of+Finance.htm.
7. As a result, implementation of reforms began in June 2006.

8. Indonesia took a gradual approach and subsequently implemented organizational reform with the establishment of a new directorate general, merging the two existing directorates managing different parts of the government debt.

9. See, for example, World Bank (2000).

10. The completion point under the Heavily Indebted Poor Countries Initiative refers to the point at which lenders are expected to provide the promised full debt relief.

11. The Public Expenditure Management and Financial Accountability Reform program is supported by a large group of donors, including the IMF and the World Bank. Its main purpose is to build capacity in the ministry of finance and it consists of 12 components, one of which is debt management.

12. The Financial Sector Reform and Strengthening Initiative is a multidonor program, supporting capacity building and policy development projects in the financial sector.

13. PHARE BG9909-02-01. Phare stands for *Pologne et Hongrie Assistance à la Reconstruction Economique.* It is an EU program established in 1989 to channel financial and technical assistance to countries in Central and Eastern Europe. The World Bank is supporting the debt management component.

14. The central bank in Sri Lanka continues to play a prominent role in debt management, and is currently building capacity under a program supported by the Asian Development Bank and the Swedish International Development Agency.

15. For example, debt management can fall under the following categories:
    - Financial sector: public debt often dominates the domestic financial markets, and the way in which it is managed has a significant impact on the efficiency of market operations.
    - Public expenditure management: interest payments are an important component of public expenditure.
    - Governance and public sector reform: debt management is conducted by the ministry of finance, the central bank, or other public institutions requiring a sound governance framework.
    - Macroeconomics: sound debt management is a contributor to macroeconomic stability and is necessary to ensure that public finances are sustainable.

16. Some basic indicators on public debt management are being tracked in the Country and Policy Institutional Assessment and the Public Expenditure and Financial Accountability Performance Measurement Framework. The Country and Policy Institutional Assessment measures the extent to which a country's current policy and institutional framework is conducive to fostering sustainable, poverty-reducing growth and the effective use of development assistance. This exercise is done annually for all International Bank for Reconstruction and Development and International Development Association borrowers. The relevant criteria are grouped into four clusters: economic

management, structural policies, policies for social inclusion and equity, and public sector management and institutions. The number of criteria, currently 16, reflects a balance between ensuring that all key factors that foster pro-poor growth and poverty alleviation are captured, without overly burdening the evaluation process.

The Public Expenditure and Financial Accountability Performance Measurement Framework was developed to contribute to the collective efforts of many stakeholders to assess and develop essential public financial management systems. The framework does this by providing a common pool of information for measurement and monitoring of public financial management performance progress and a common platform for dialogue.

CHAPTER 3

1. These broader issues will be discussed in subsequent chapters. Individual country case reports under the pilot program provide a more detailed description of the debt composition and macroeconomic context within which each country managed its debt portfolio. See also table 1.1 in chapter 1.
2. Under the current definition, external debt refers to debt contracted in the international capital markets or from commercial, multilateral, and bilateral creditors. Domestic debt refers to debt contracted in the domestic market and other domestic sources and can include debt denominated in foreign currency. The domestic debt can also be purchased by foreign investors.
3. Forced placements typically help governments reduce cost and extend the average maturity of the domestic debt in the short run, but are not conducive to the medium-term goal of developing the domestic debt market.
4. Concessional loans are loans extended by creditors at below-market terms.
5. Central Bank of Sri Lanka 2002.
6. This should be distinguished from management of subportfolios that is consistent with the cost and risk objectives for the overall debt portfolio. In fact, a target for the subportfolio, such as targets for the domestic and foreign-currency portfolios, helps better guide portfolio managers' actions aimed at managing risks in the respective markets.
7. For example, in Colombia in 2001, the Debt Directorate sought to pre-fund external borrowing for 2002—a presidential election year, which was expected to complicate the issuance process in international capital markets. However, the Debt Directorate could not get complete approval from the National Council of Economic and Social Policy to undertake the external transactions because of the National Planning Department's concerns that these transactions would increase the debt servicing burden, which would, in turn, crowd out resources for investment. In the end, the Debt Directorate was unable to pre-finance the full amount for which it requested authorization.
8. Without ranges, debt managers would be forced to rebalance their portfolios very frequently for even the smallest moves in markets. In countries where

macroeconomic instability and capital flow volatilities are a major factor, or where strategy development is still at an incipient stage, "soft" targets with broader ranges than the Bulgarian case might be more appropriate than narrower ranges.

9. http://www.minhacienda.gov.co/pls/portal30/docs/FOLDER/ REPOSITORIO/CONFIS/DOC/FINANCIERO/DOC+-+0005+ -+2005.PDF.

10. The share of domestic debt in overall debt portfolios must be interpreted with caution. The increase in the share of domestic debt in the overall debt portfolios of Bulgaria and Colombia was the result of a reduction in foreign-currency debt and stable domestic-currency debt (as a share of GDP). In Kenya, however, it was due to an increase in domestic debt relative to foreign-currency debt as a percentage of GDP, partly due to the lack of access to donor funding for budget support. The increase in the share of domestic-currency debt in total debt in Nicaragua and Zambia was due to a large reduction in foreign-currency debt following the Heavily Indebted Poor Countries process. Croatia's share of domestic debt in total debt changed little over 2002–04, but it has increased more recently as part of the new government debt management strategy to reduce the external debt share and develop the domestic government debt market.

11. Indonesia only began domestic borrowing after 1997, to recapitalize banks after the crisis. Initially, domestic bonds were placed directly with banks, but since 2002 the government has been issuing domestic bonds through auctions.

12. The Colombian authority has moved aggressively to raise the relative share of the domestic debt in the overall debt portfolio and improve its profile through transactions that include
   • debt exchanges, which have allowed them to extend maturities in the domestic market and in some cases switch from external debt to domestic debt in the process;
   • prepayment of external debt (by issuing TES to buy US dollars from the central bank with which to prepay external debt);
   • issuance of international bonds denominated in Colombian pesos; and
   • foreign-to-domestic-currency-swap transactions.

13. As a result, the weighted average time to maturity of the domestic-currency debt portfolio rose from 5.3 years to 6.9 years, with debt maturing within the next 12 months declining from 5 percent to less than 1 percent, and the share of fixed-rate debt rising from 70 percent to 83 percent between 2002 and 2005.

14. Previously in Lebanon, the authorities acted to contain the vulnerabilities to adverse interest rate and exchange rate changes by negotiating a refinancing package with the international community, domestic banks, and the central bank (Paris II Conference). This led to a reduction in debt servicing costs and reduced rollover and interest-rate risks in the portfolio.

CHAPTER 4

1. This amounted to an increase from 12.7 percent of GDP in 2001 to 17.9 percent in 2002.
2. As of 2006, the debt directorate in the Ministry of Finance of Costa Rica carries out its own debt sustainability analysis.
3. Fiscal sustainability analysis is frequently conducted and reported by the World Bank and IMF.
4. In Lebanon, the central bank assumed responsibility for domestic debt management because capacity in the ministry of finance deteriorated as a result of the prolonged civil war. More recently, the central bank has acted as agent for the ministry of finance.
5. Central banks' poor balance sheet positions have been attributed to the need to offset underfinancing of deficits by the government and to their role as lenders of last resort. The negative cost of carry between the yield on assets and liabilities has also contributed to the accumulation of liabilities. The cost of monetary operations, including the quasi-fiscal deficits generated by the central bank, must ultimately be borne by the government. See IMF (2004b).
6. If payments are missed, even for one day, rating agencies consider it a default. For example, Standard & Poor's generally defines default as the failure to meet a principal or interest payment on the due date (or within a specified grace period) contained in the original terms of the debt issue. An issuer's debt is considered in default in any of the following circumstances:
   - For local and foreign-currency bonds, notes, and bills, when either scheduled debt service is not paid on the due date, or an exchange offer of new debt has terms less favorable than those of the original issue.
   - For central bank currency, when notes are converted into new currency of less than equivalent face value.
   - For bank loans, when either scheduled debt service is not paid on the due date, or a rescheduling of principal or interest (or both) is agreed to by creditors at less favorable terms than those of the original loan.

   Such rescheduling agreements covering short- and long-term bank debt are considered defaults even where, for legal or regulatory reasons, creditors consider forced rollover of principal to be voluntary. In addition, many rescheduled sovereign bank loans are ultimately extinguished at a discount from their original face value. Typical deals have included exchange offers (such as those linked to the issuance of Brady bonds), debt-equity swaps related to government privatization programs, and buybacks for cash. Standard & Poor's considers such transactions defaults when they feature terms less favorable than those of the original obligation.
7. The debt-to-GDP ratio started diminishing from 2004 onward.
8. The initial buildup of debt is the result of various factors, including declining domestic growth (Colombia, Costa Rica, Croatia); lax fiscal policy (Costa Rica, Croatia); costs of civil war and reconstruction (Lebanon, Sri Lanka); the

realization of contingent debt (Lebanon); and snowballing of debt owing to high debt servicing costs (Croatia, Costa Rica, Lebanon, Sri Lanka).

9. Following the Paris II Conference of the international community, the government of Lebanon received low-interest loans from a number of sources and improved the risk profile of its public debt. The country also enjoyed favorable external conditions during the period—with declining world interest rates and capital inflows resulting in an expanding deposit base in the banking system. However, vulnerabilities relating to the size of the public debt remained large.

10. The debt relief helped lower debt levels from 213 percent of GDP at the end of 2003 to 93 percent in 2004 (or from 173.5 percent to 70.0 percent in net present value terms).

11. In Costa Rica, by 2004, the debt-to-GDP ratio had risen to 60 percent from 46 percent in 1999. In Croatia, the ratio climbed to 42 percent from 27 percent in 1998.

12. In Bulgaria, macroeconomic stability with low inflation and improving fiscal performance—the result of a tight expenditure policy and revenue overperformance coupled with high economic growth—helped reduce debt to 35 percent of GDP in 2005 from 80 percent in 2000. In Indonesia, the financial crisis of the late 1990s left the government with a large increase in debt, to 108 percent of GDP in 2000 from 23 percent before the crisis. The government debt ratio has since gradually fallen, owing mainly to GDP growth, and was approaching 50 percent of GDP at the end of 2005. In Tunisia, the central-government-debt-to-GDP ratio declined slightly to 51.7 percent in 2005 from 52.1 percent in 2001.

13. See *Developing the Domestic Government Debt Market*.

14. See *Developing the Domestic Government Debt Market* for a discussion of the implications of multiple issuers for domestic government debt market development.

15. In the absence of well-designed governance arrangements for monetary policy, similar pressure might also be placed on the monetary authorities, to the detriment of their price stability objectives.

16. From the standpoint of overall net worth, it makes little difference where the liabilities lie because the central bank is owned by the government. The debate occurs because the government is more visibly accountable for its fiscal deficit, usually a cash measure that does not capture the losses of the central bank.

CHAPTER 5

1. These ceilings, however, function more as a means to control the budget than to influence debt management directly.

2. Specifically, the regulation authorized the DMO in the finance ministry to "make credit arrangements and implement the issue of bonds on the domestic and foreign securities markets, as well as manage the portfolio of public

debt with regard to their sources, deadlines, currency, and interest structure, and propose measures and instruments to minimize the risks and costs of repayments." It also specifies the responsibility for keeping records on the debt and to "monitor the obligations of the State, prepare estimates of the amounts for repayment of domestic and foreign debts, review the accuracy of the calculated obligations and monitor their regular payments."

3. In Tunisia, the debt ceiling, expressed as a percentage of GDP, is defined in the five-year plan developed by the ministry of development and international cooperation.

4. Since the budget of 2005, parliamentary approval has been modified to net terms.

5. Tunisia had a similar practice until the late 1990s. At the time, the annual finance law established individual limits for internal and external debt. If one of those limits was exceeded, but overall borrowing stayed within the approved limit, the following year's finance law could legalize the situation. The law thus did not block the operation of the treasury as long as overall net financing did not exceed the ceiling approved by the national assembly. This system of individual limits was replaced by a net limit on total government borrowing that gave the treasury greater discretion to choose between debt instruments in accordance with the debt management strategy.

6. However, each individual guarantee must be approved by Congress.

7. Such risks include errors, fraud, data loss, and business disruption, attributable to inadequate controls and policy breaches that have the potential to generate large losses for the government and to tarnish the reputation of debt managers.

8. The International Organization of Supreme Audit Institutions Public Debt Committee has developed several guidelines in recent years. In reviewing these guidelines, it realized that the guidelines assumed that appropriate systems of debt accounting, management, and reporting were in place, which may not be true of all developing countries. The Zambian Supreme Audit Institution therefore requested that committee give special consideration to the applicability of the guidelines when systems of debt accounting, management, and reporting are not strong. The committee decided to use the Zambian experience as a test case. Accordingly, the Zambian Supreme Audit Institution was requested to review the applicability of the developed guidelines in their country and report the findings as a case study. See http://www.intosaipdc.org.mx/nuevos_ingles/i0012ipdc.PDF.

9. A procedures manual provides an official guide outlining how to perform many of the routine operations that confront the DMO, including for the front office, procedures for transacting in the market and entering the transactions; and for the back office, procedures for transaction verification, database maintenance, and debt servicing.

10. Because bond issuance tended to be sporadic, this source of information was not regular and the information could become quickly outdated. In addition

to the requirements of credit rating agencies, the disclosure requirements for borrowing in some jurisdictions (such as New York) are greater and have resulted in some uniformity of disclosure across countries.

11. See http://www.minfin.government.bg/inpage.php?id=215&language =english.

12. See http://www.centralbanklanka.org/Public%20Debt_Mgt.pdf.

13. Serious operational problems arose with relation to an external debt swap because the front office did not notify the back office of a swap from euro to US dollars, and the back office made debt servicing payments in euro. Because of the swap incident, coordination is now improved: when a major transaction is to be made (for example, bond with a swap), all the front-, middle-, and back-office units meet to discuss the implications of the transaction and all units are thus adequately informed.

CHAPTER 6

1. In Kenya, staff left for the private sector and for a donor-funded, regional, capacity-building provider.

2. This program was discontinued, however, when Colombia experienced the worst budget deficit of the century, which resulted in the cancellation of all training programs.

3. In countries where the central bank has no control over monetary policy—for example, those that are members of a monetary union—the central bank can be a perfectly legitimate place to conduct debt management operations.

4. A UNDP-funded project (Capacity Development for Fiscal Reform and Management) was set up in the mid-1990s to build capacity in the finance ministry across a range of areas—including tax reform, expenditure management, customs reform, and public debt management.

5. AusAID provided targeted capacity-building assistance under a four-year program that combined seminars and workshops, on-the-job training, and use of external consultants as external advisors working with the Indonesian staff (AusAID 2004).

6. For a discussion on the pros and cons of a separate debt management office, see, for example, Currie, Dithier, and Togo (2003).

7. Even if the database is unified, downloading to separate software from the debt recording system for analytical purpose is nevertheless good practice because it helps ensure that the debt database is protected and prevents contamination by other users.

8. A project to ensure easy access to consolidated data is under way.

9. In Colombia, the treasury and public credit office were consolidated into one entity during the pilot program.

10. For example, the World Bank requires its borrowers to provide accurate and timely debt statistics as a condition for making new loans. Article III, Section 4, in the Bank's Articles of Agreement states

    "... the Bank shall pay due regard to the prospects that the borrower ... will be in a position to meet its obligations under the loan." The "General Conditions Applicable to Loan and Guarantee Agreements" state that borrowers must furnish information with respect to financial and economic conditions in their countries, including data on external debt.

11. An incident involving a foreign-currency swap described in footnote 13 in chapter 5 related to poor communication between the front and back offices, and the lack of established procedures for entering and monitoring swap transactions.

12. According to UNCTAD, some countries in Latin America, including Argentina, Bolivia, Ecuador, Guatemala, and Panama, have linked DMFAS to the public financial management system.

13. As part of the implementation of reforms, the authorities decided to acquire a new system.

14. A sample survey of six Organisation for Economic Co-operation and Development countries suggests that the budget allocated for systems (including salaries) accounts for an average of 20 percent of annual operating expenditures (OECD 2002b).

15. Indeed, a number of Organisation for Economic Co-operation and Development countries have done the same in response to limitations within their own core public service.

16. Specific measures include temporary placements of central bank or private sector personnel in the debt management unit, or the use of longer-term advisors with specialist skills in public debt management.

REFERENCES

AusAID (Australian Agency for International Development). 2004. "Indonesia Debt Management Project: Activity Completion Report." Canberra, Australia.

Bulgaria Ministry of Finance. 2003. "Government Debt Management Strategy." Sofia, Bulgaria. Available at http://www.minfin.government.bg/docs/dd25-01e.pdf.

———. 2005. "Government Debt Monthly Bulletin." January.

Central Bank of Kenya. 2001. "Monthly Economic Review–July." Nairobi, Kenya.

———. 2005. "Monthly Economic Review – October." Nairobi, Kenya.

Central Bank of Sri Lanka. 2003. *Annual Report 2002.* Colombo.

Colombia Ministry of Finance and Public Credit. n. d. Deuda Publica. Excel document. http://www.minhacienda.gov.co/portal/page?_pageid=9,620,9_1812&_dad=portal30&_schema=PORTAL30.

Croatia Ministry of Finance. 2005. "Monthly Statistical Review." June. Bureau for Macroeconomic Analysis and Planning, Zagreb, Croatia. Available at http://www.mfin.hr/str/67/.

Currie, Elizabeth, Jean Jacques Dithier, and Eriko Togo. 2003. "Institutional Arrangements for Public Debt Management." World Bank Policy Research Working Paper No. 3021, Washington, DC.

Dornbusch, Rudi. 2001. "A Primer on Emerging Market Crises." NBER Working Paper No. 8326, National Bureau for Economic Research, Cambridge, MA.

Frankel, Jeffrey, and Shan-Jin Wei. 2005. "Managing Macroeconomic Crises: Policy Lessons." In *Managing Economic Volatility and Crises: A Practitioner's Guide,* ed. Joshua Aizenman and Brian Pinto. New York: Cambridge University Press.

IMF (International Monetary Fund). 2000. "Code of Good Practices on Transparency in Monetary and Financial Policies." Washington, DC.

———. 2001. "Code of Good Practices on Fiscal Transparency." Washington, DC. Available at http://www.imf.org/np/fad/trans/code.htm#code.

———. 2003. "Costa Rica: 2002 Article IV Consultation." Washington, DC

———. 2004a. "Lebanon, Report on Interim Staff Visit." Washington, DC.

———. 2004b. "Monetary Policy Implementation at Different Stages of Market Development." Monetary and Financial Systems Department, Washington, DC.

———. 2004c. "Pakistan: 2004 Article IV Consultation." IMF Country Report No. 04/411, Washington, DC.

———. 2004d. "Republic of Croatia, 2004 Article IV Consultation and Request for Standby Arrangement—Staff Report." IMF Country Report No. 04/253, Washington, DC.

———. 2005a. "Financial Sector Assessment Program: Review, Lessons, and Issues Going Forward." Washington, DC.

———. 2005b. "Indonesia, 2005 Article IV Consultation." IMF Country Report No. 05/326, Washington, DC.

———. 2005c. "Poverty Reduction Strategy Paper." IMF Country Report 05/11, Washington, DC.

———. 2006a. "Report on the Evaluation of the Financial Sector Assessment Program." Independent Evaluation Office, Washington, DC.

———. 2006b. *World Economic Outlook*. Washington, DC.

———. 2006c. "Zambia: Selected Issues and Statistical Appendix." IMF Country Report 06/118, Washington, DC.

Indonesia Ministry of Finance. 2005. Central Government Debt Statistical Tables, Quarter I.

International Organization of Supreme Audit Institutions. 2000. "Guidance for Planning and Conducting an Audit of Internal Controls of Public Debt." Public Debt Committee. www.intosai.org.

Nicaragua Ministry of Finance. n.d. Serie Historica de las relaciones de la deuda externa e internal del gobierno central con respecto a los indicadores economicos.

OECD (Organisation for Economic Co-operation and Development). 2002a. *Debt Management and Government Securities Markets in the 21st Century*. Paris: OECD.

———. 2002b. "Report on Operational Risk Management of Government Debt," Working Party on Government Debt Management.

SIDA (Swedish International Development Cooperation Agency). 1996. *Debt Management (Kenya): Swedish Support to the Ministry of Finance*. SIDA Evaluation Series 96/2, Stockholm.

Sri Lanka. 2001. "Focus Group on Public Debt Management, Final Report." June 13.

Wheeler, Graeme. 2004. *Sound Practice in Government Debt Management*. Washington, DC: World Bank.

World Bank. 1996. "World Bank Technical Assistance: Lessons and Practices." Operations Evaluation Department, No. 7, Washington, DC.

———. 2000. *Reforming Public Institutions and Strengthening Governance: A World Bank Strategy*. Washington, DC.

———. 2001. "Bulgaria: The Dual Challenge of Transition and European Union Accession." Poverty Reduction and Economic Management Unit, Europe and Central Asia Region, Washington, DC.

————. 2003a. *Bulgaria: Public Expenditure Issues and Directions for Reform.* Washington, DC.

————. 2003b. "Public Financial Management: Scaling Up from Diagnostics to Capacity Development." Unpublished, Washington, DC.

————. 2004a. "Program Document: A Proposed Second Programmatic Adjustment Loan in the Amount of Euro 123.7 Million to the Republic of Bulgaria." Washington, DC.

————. 2004b. "Republic of Tunisia: Strategy for Public Debt Management." Washington, DC.

————. 2005. "Improving Public Sector Governance: The Grand Challenge?" In *Economic Growth in the 1990s: Learning from a Decade of Reform.* Washington, DC.

————. 2006. *World Development Indicators.* Washington, DC.

————. Articles of Agreement, http://web.worldbank.org/WBSITE/ EXTERNAL/EXTABOUTUS/ORGANIZATION/BODEXT/0,, contentMDK:20049557~menuPK:64020045~pagePK:64020054 ~piPK:64020408~theSitePK:278036,00.html.

World Bank and IMF. 2001a. *Developing Government Bond Markets: A Handbook.* Washington, DC.

————. 2001b. "Guidelines for Public Debt Management." Washington, DC.

————. 2003a. "Accompanying Document to Guidelines for Public Debt Management." Washington, DC.

————. 2003b. "Financial Sector Assessment Program: Review, Lessons, and Issues Going Forward." Washington, DC.

INDEX

Printed in the United States
146734LV00004B/2/A

9 780821 368725